COOK

BOOK

2314

ADAM
BLUE

Stone House Press
247 Burr Road
Cornish, NH 03745

First Printing: 2014

ISBN: 1500262854
ISBN-13: 978-1500262853

This book is lovingly dedicated
to my family.

Forward

Curious isn't it, living after the end of history.

Because the end of history was the end of society—and society ended wrong, ripe with mutation and infighting. The darkest instinct for survival became the only logic left, if you hoped to see tomorrow.

Yet through food, the vestiges of our humanity persist. So simple, this fundamental daily process—who would have thought that the act of nourishing our bodies would be the final refuge for our souls?

It seems our leaders, the champions that they are with sawed-off shotguns, do find some aesthetic pleasure in the violence that's their charge. So perhaps we're more misguided than lost. I don't know. I just couldn't walk away fast enough.

For me, in breaking bread our lives are affirmed once more. Our relationships with each other, the planet, our past—each can find some light, some breath, and be awakened. Communion at long last. I think you know what I mean.

Be well,

~ab.

August 2314
The Eastern Range

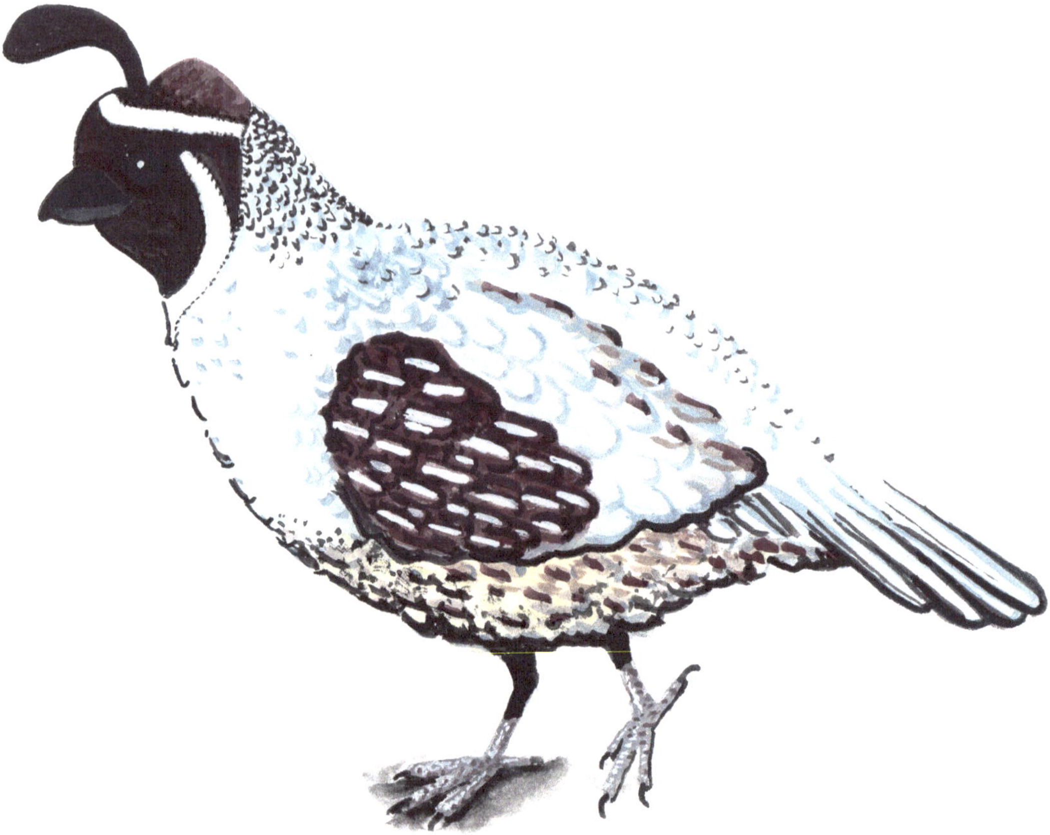

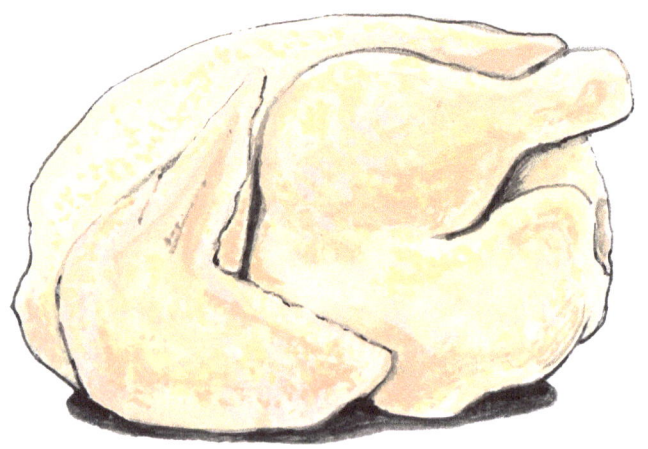

Gambler's Quail

Though no longer as plentiful as they once were, Gambler's Quail can still be found in the rocky prairies north of the Old High Road. As unaware as they are delicious, these handsome birds are easily caught in Hennicker's traps. The "gamble" in their name comes from collecting them—as there's great risk in every moment spent on the open plains. Though the lurkers have no taste for the quail proper, they've realized that a loaded trap is an ideal site to catch one of us.

Roasted Quail with Umbrella Mushroom Stuffing
Serves two

- 2 Gambler's Quail
- Salt, Ground Picant, and Lemoline to taste
- 1 cup Umbrella Mushrooms, coarse cut
- ½ cup Yellow Onion, diced
- ½ teaspoon Sunflower Seed Oil
- ½ cup Weekender's Wine
- 1 Egg
- 1 cup stale Ground Picant Focaccia Crumbs

1. Start a large fire in your grill.
2. Prepare the quail with a salt, ground picant, and lemoline rub. Allow to rest until the coals are ready.
3. To prepare the stuffing: in a separate pan, sauté onions in sunflower seed oil until translucent. Add umbrella mushrooms and cook until mushrooms are tender and browned. Add weekender's wine; reduce the liquid by half. Remove from heat and mix into breadcrumbs, egg, salt and ground picant to taste.
4. Fill the body cavity of the Gambler's Quail with the stuffing. Set on grill, cooking covered with indirect heat for forty-five minutes, or until done. Quail skin should be golden brown with juices running clear and the meat should be firm to the touch.

Bigote

These tasty fish are common in lakes and slow-moving sections of rivers, as tangled reeds and mud are their preferred habitat. They'll eat pretty much anything, so fishing for Bigote is fun and easy. I've had luck casting leftovers onto the water, waiting with a net for when they rise to eat. As attractive as a dinner filled with their sweet, flaky meat can be, taking children fishing for Bigote is even better. Their wet, slimy antics quickly become hysterical for everyone, feeding your spirit as well as your body.

Spicy Bigote with Traveler's Peppers and Yellow Onions
Serves two
- 2 Bigote fillets
- Salt, Ground Picant, and Garlic Powder to taste
- A dusting of Golden Wheat Flour
- 2 tablespoons Sunflower Seed Oil
- 1 Yellow Onion, sliced into rings
- 1 Traveler's Pepper, sliced into strips
- 1 Green Bell Pepper, sliced into strips

1. Start a medium wood fire in your grill.
2. Season fish with salt, ground picant, and garlic powder to taste. Dust lightly with flour and set aside.
3. Heat sunflower seed oil in a large pan over medium-low coals. Add onions and peppers. Stir occasionally for twenty minutes, until toppings have caramelized. Salt and ground picant to taste. Remove from pan and set vegetable topping aside.
4. Add fish to now-flavored oil in pan and set over hot coals. Cook until the fish is opaque throughout and the flour coating begins to brown, about four minutes per side.
5. Transfer fish to plates and smother with onions and peppers before serving.

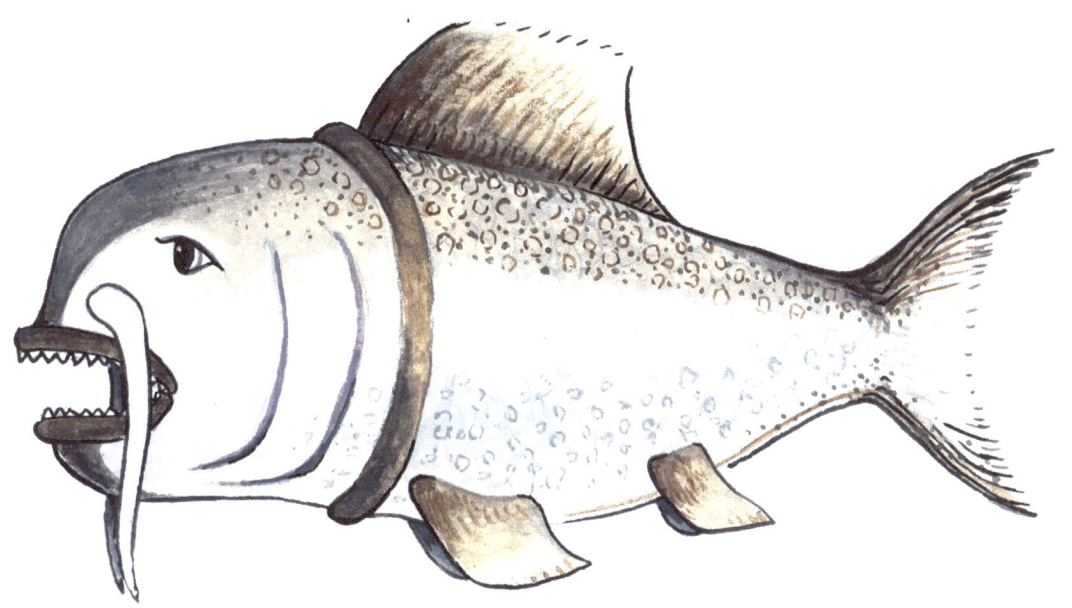

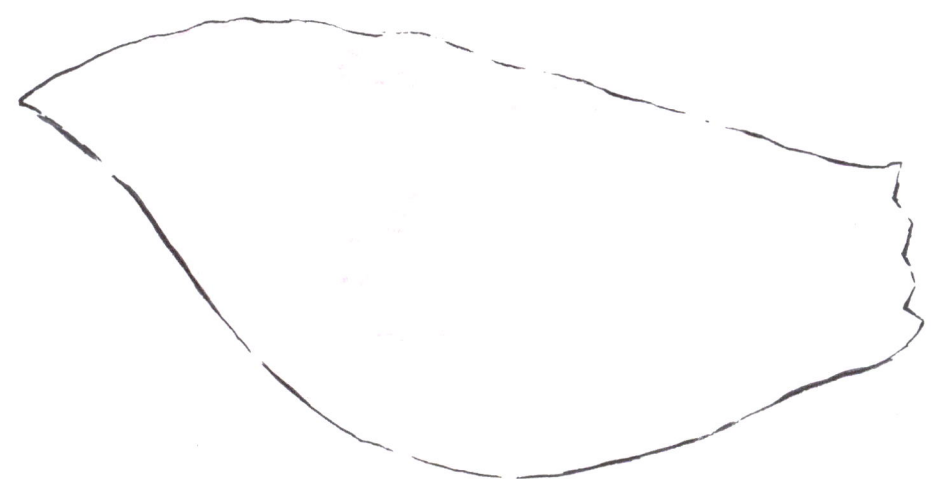

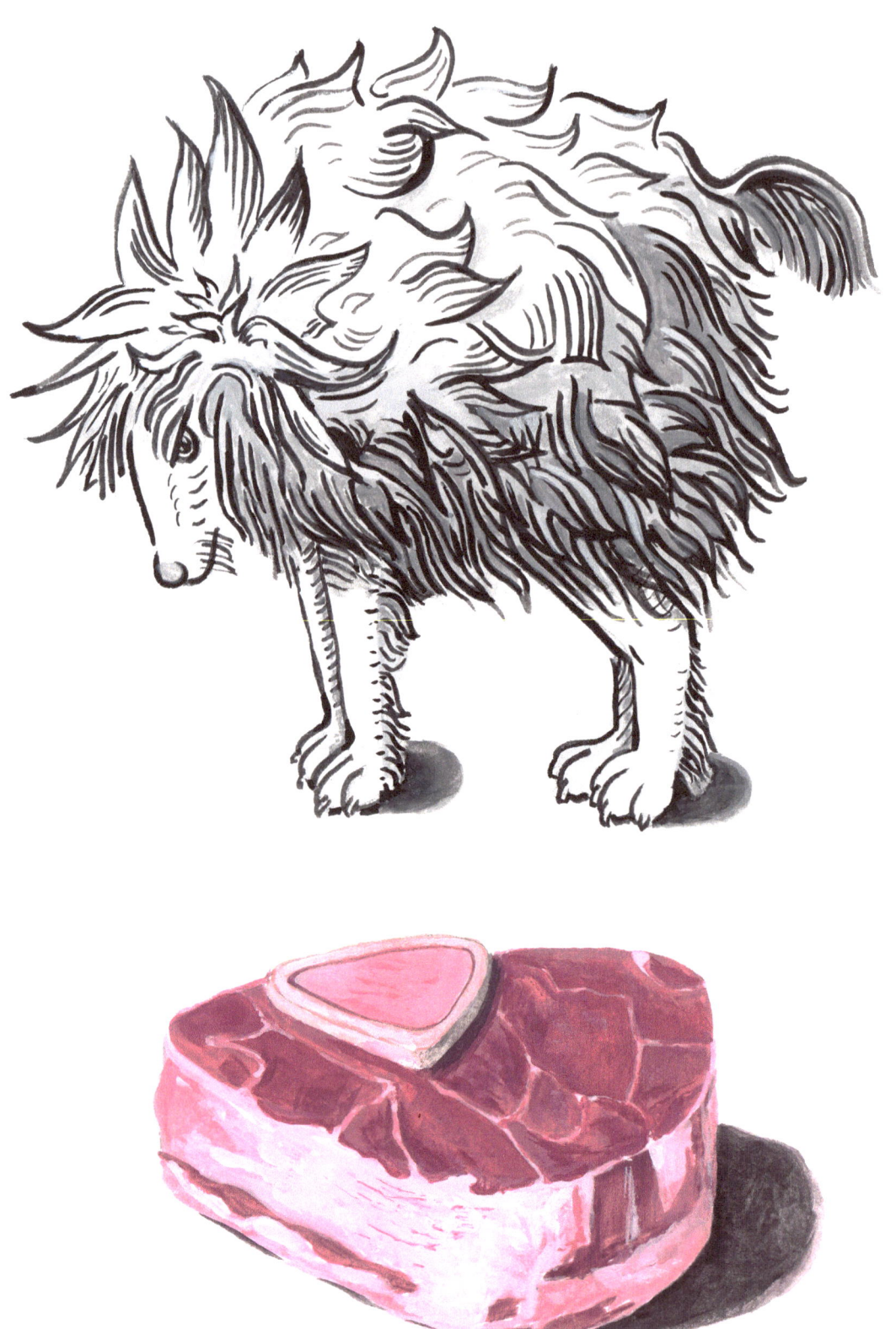

Sheep-Wolf

If language, in its own way, helps create our reality, then we got what our ancestors deserved. Once mythical creatures, Sheep-Wolf now slip into our flocks, obscured until it's too late for one of our sheep. These nasty predators are difficult to track and harder to hunt, so if you plan to celebrate with a Sheep-Wolf dish, try trading with the Shephards of the Crescent Mountains when they pass through. From my experience, Sheep-Wolf meat tends to be gamey and tough in the spring. But by the fall, their successful summer hunt makes their meat fuller, fattier, and more flavorful.

Sheep-Wolf Stew
Serves four
- 2 tablespoons of Sunflower Seed Oil
- 2 pounds Sheep-Wolf, cut into bite-sized cubes
- Salt and Ground Picant to taste
- A dusting of Golden Wheat Flour
- Dry spices to taste: Bay Leaf, Thyme, and Mustard Seed
- 2 medium Yellow Onions, diced
- 3 cups Chicken Stock
- 4 Gemstone Potatoes, cubed
- 4 Ghostroot, cut into wheels
- ½ cup Brandy
- Fresh herbs to taste: Parsley and Lemoline

1. Prepare a large fire in the grill and allow the coals to settle.
2. Heat sunflower seed oil in a large pot over medium-high heat.
3. Roll cubed meat in salt and ground picant, dust with flour. Cook meat in oil until browned on all sides, about eight minutes.
4. Move pot to medium heat. Add onions and cook until transparent.
5. Add stock and dry spices. Bring to a boil. Reduce heat and simmer uncovered for twenty minutes.
6. Add potatoes and ghostroot. Simmer uncovered to cook vegetables until fork-tender, while also reducing and thickening sauce, about forty-five minutes. Add brandy with five minutes remaining.
7. If necessary, thicken stock with roux made from additional flour. Add fresh herbs as garnish.

Giant Waterbeetle

Common to the rice paddies of the Westerlands, Giant Waterbeetles grow to intimidating size, don't bite or sting, and—contrary to their looks—are quite tasty. They're simple to catch after dark, as they can't resist swimming towards bright lights. Once in the kitchen, Giant Waterbeetles can be roasted or fried, with both processes bringing out their sweet, nutty flavors. Remember to remove the head and outer wings to keep them tender.

Grilled Chicken with Chili Sauce
Serves four

- 1 Chicken, quartered
- 1 Lime, Zest and Juice
- Salt to taste
- 2 cloves Garlic, minced
- ½ cup Honey
- 1 Giant Waterbeetle, ground
- 1 Traveler's Pepper, diced
- ¼ cup fresh Lemoline, Cilantro, and toasted Sunflower Seeds

1. Build a large, hot fire for cooking uncovered over direct heat.
2. Prepare the chicken with a rub made from one chopped garlic clove, lime zest, and salt. Once the coals are ready, grill the chicken for about forty-five minutes, flipping the meat four times. The chicken is done when juices run clear and the meat is firm to the touch.
3. While the chicken is cooking, make your chili glaze. Begin by removing the giant waterbeetle's head and outer wings. Crush the body with side of your knife and chop it into smaller pieces. Combine it with the diced traveler's pepper, honey, and lime juice in mortar and pestle and work together to create the basting glaze.
4. When the chicken is nearly done, brush glaze onto meat and continue cooking for five minutes. Flip meat one final time, apply glaze to other side and grill for five minutes.
5. Garnish with lemoline, cilantro, and sunflower seeds before serving.

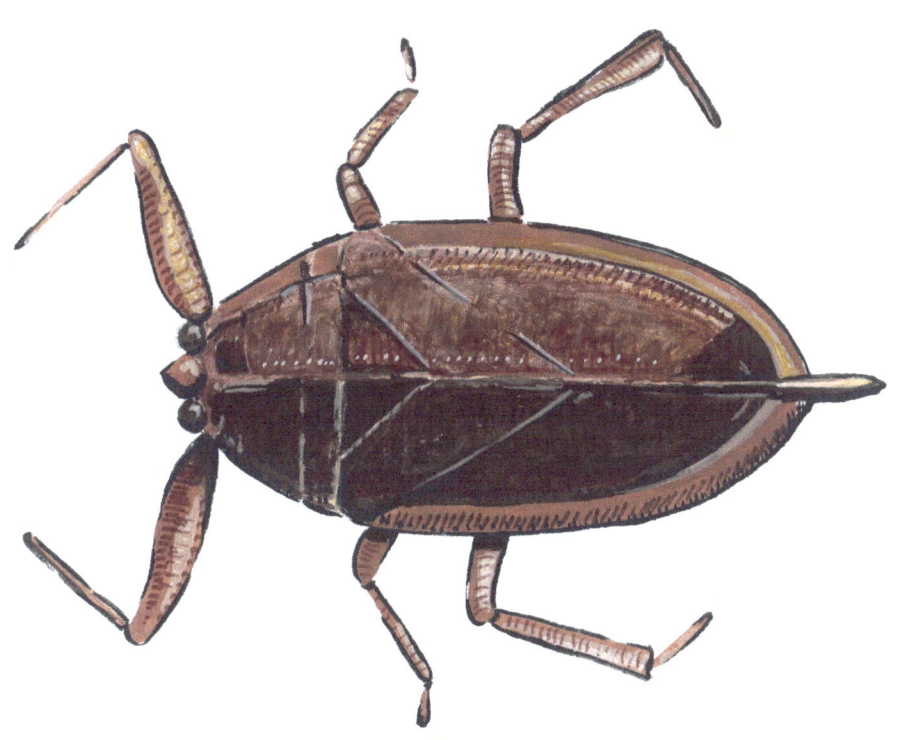

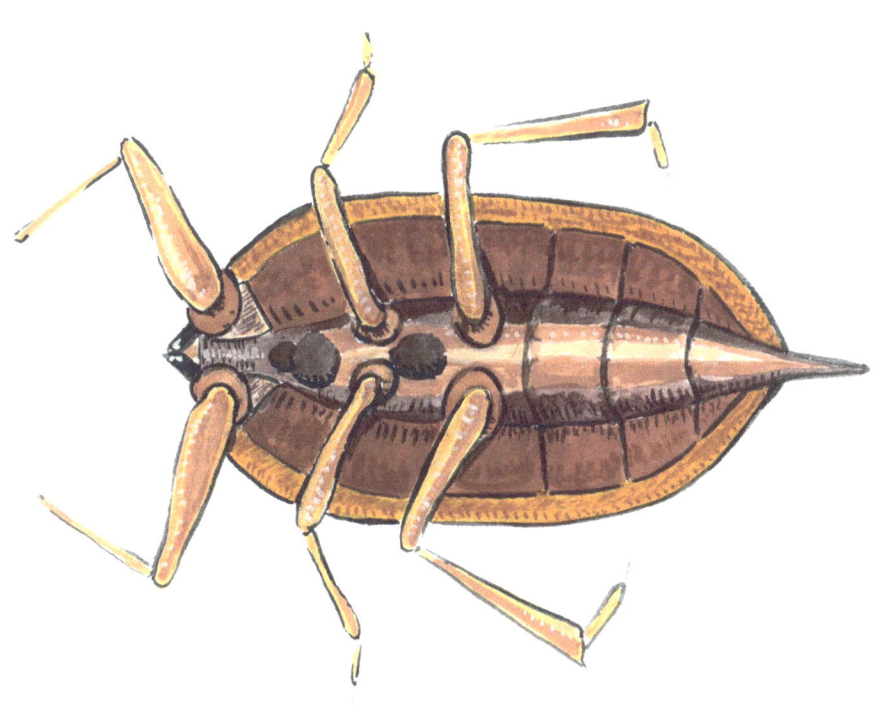

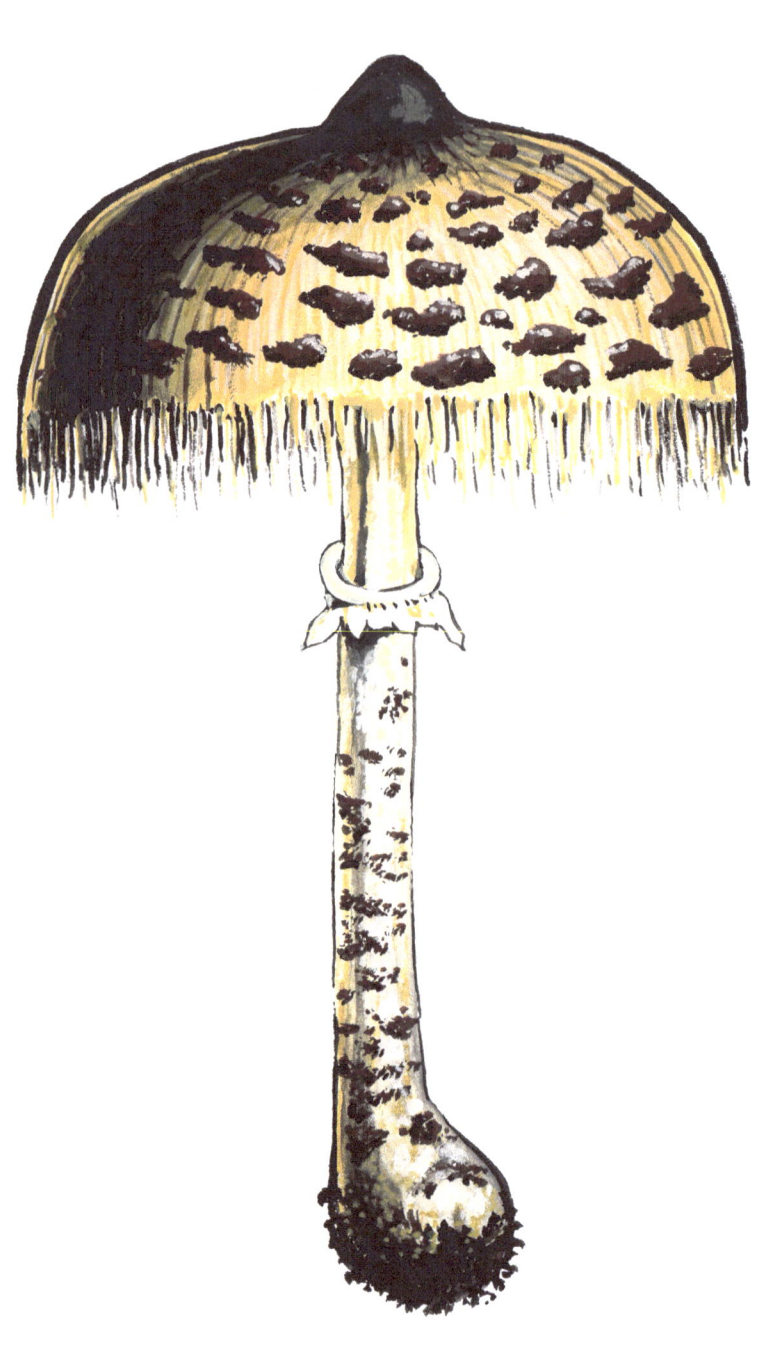

Umbrella Mushroom

These large, fleshy mushrooms have a distinctive flavor that takes marinades well, making them a longtime vegetarian staple. Umbrella Mushrooms are easy to identify and quick to forage, as every spring they emerge in the same place. If you're disciplined about never picking more than half of what you find, you'll have a sustainable patch to enjoy for life. Look for them on the northeast side of moss-covered logs in mixed-species forests.

Umbrella Mushroom Soup
Serves four

- 2 cups Umbrella Mushrooms, diced
- 2 tablespoons Butter
- ½ Yellow Onion, diced
- 2 Celery sticks, diced
- 1 large Ghostroot, diced
- 4 cups Chicken Stock
- 1 cup Cream
- Salt and Ground Picant to taste
- 16 Ground Picant Focaccia Croutons
- 2 tablespoons Parsley, chopped

1. Build a medium-sized fire in your grill.
2. In a large pot, sauté onion, celery, and ghostroot in butter over medium-low heat until they are soft and their texture starts to break down. Add diced umbrella mushrooms and cook until edges have browned and flesh is tender, but be sure they keep their shape.
3. Add chicken stock and bring to boil over high heat. Transfer to low heat and simmer uncovered for thirty minutes. Stir in cream. Simmer for an additional ten minutes. Add salt and grount picant to taste.
4. Garnish with chopped parsley and croutons and serve.

Witch's Wand

Witch's Wand is no joke: these colorful mushrooms can cause vivid hallucinations if underdone. However, when prepared correctly, they adopt a rich, caramel flavor and can gently uplift the mood of your gathering. If undercooked, it's probably best that the moon is full, that you have plenty of musical instruments and paints at hand, and that you're surrounded by close friends who have eaten them before. Worth repeating: too little is better than too much and Witches Wand is not for everyone. Then again, neither is reality.

Witch's Wand Sauce for Game Meats
Serves four
- 4 Witch's Wand Mushrooms
- 1 tablespoon Butter
- 1 Leek, cut into long strips
- 2 tablespoons sweet Weekender's Wine
- 2 cups Chicken Stock
- 1 cup Cream
- Collected drippings from roasted game meat
- 1 cup dried Golden Weekenders

1. Be sure to roast your game meat in a deep pan. When it approaches half-done, it's time to prepare the witch's wand sauce.
2. In a separate pot, melt butter over medium-high heat. Frizzle leeks and set aside.
3. Wash and separate the witch's wand caps from stems, preserving the caps whole and chopping the stems. Add to butter and cook until soft, a minimum of ten minutes. Add wine and reduce liquid by half, cooking off the alcohol and further breaking down the mushrooms in the process. Add chicken stock and cream and bring to boil.
4. Remove the finished meat from grill, transfer to a cutting board, and allow to rest while you finish the sauce.
5. Pour witch's wand sauce into meat pan, place over medium-high heat and whisk until drippings have lifted and sauce has emulsified. Reduce the sauce over low heat until it coats a spoon.
6. Carve meat. Bathe in sauce. Garnish with frizzled leeks and dried golden weekenders.

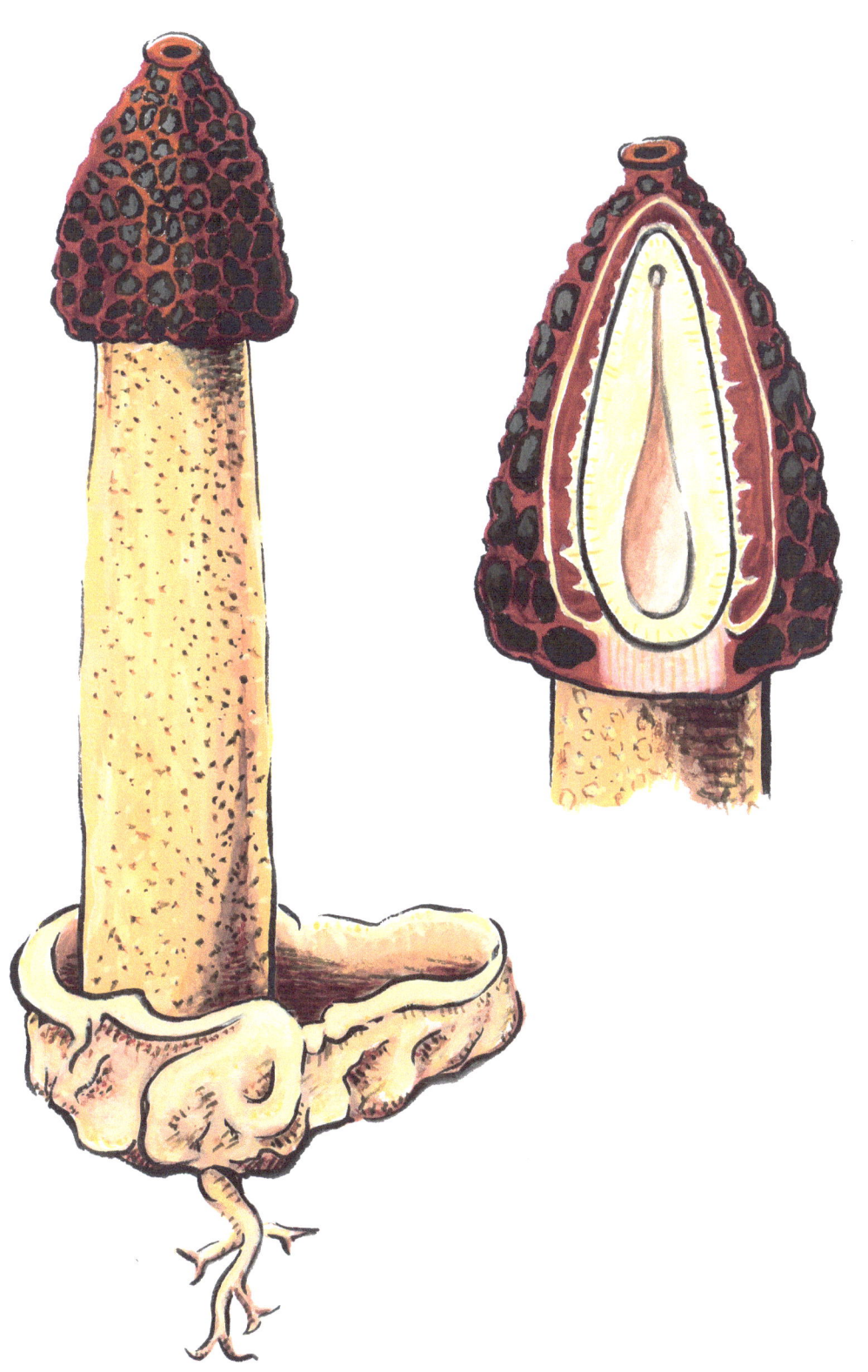

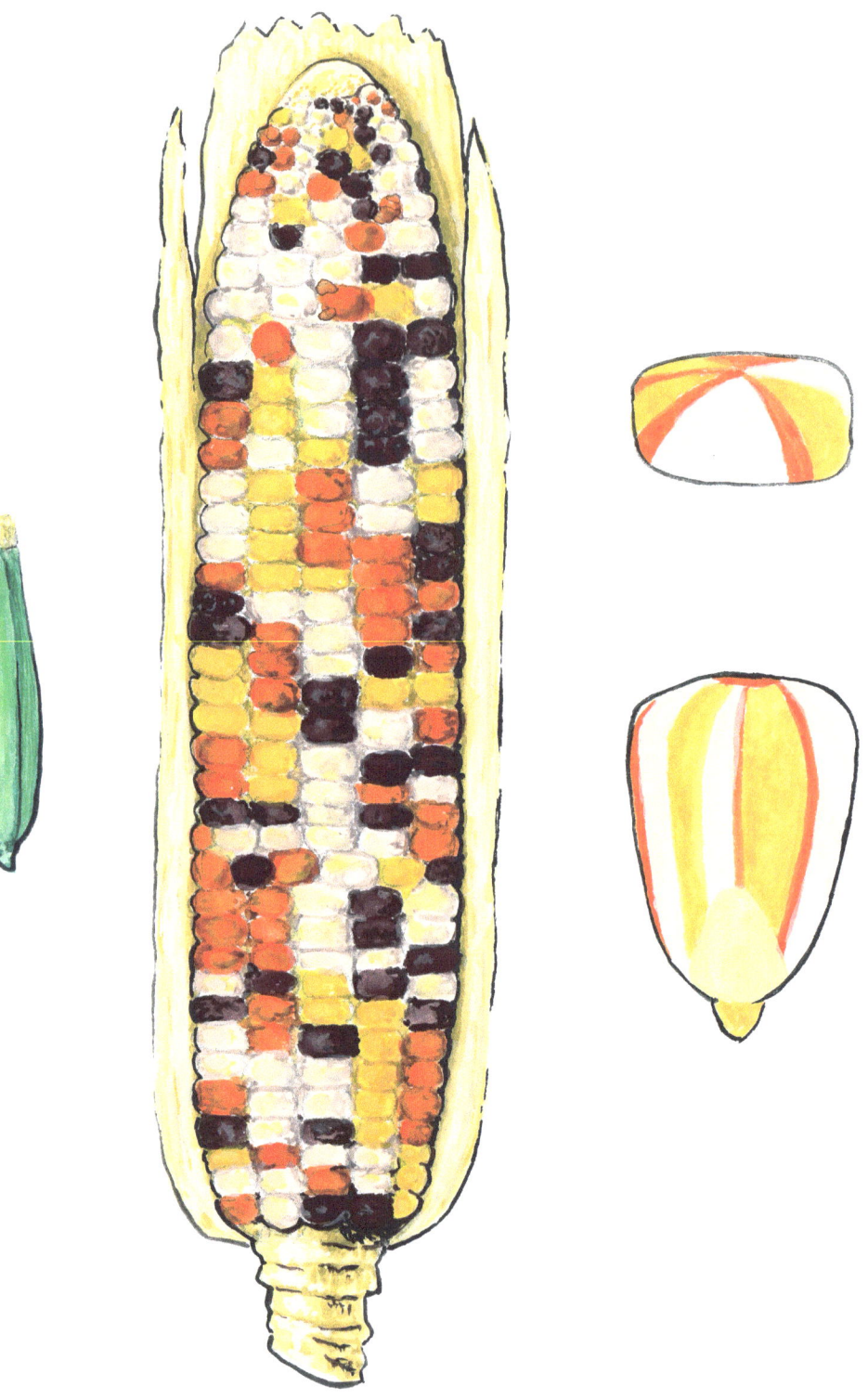

Wild Corn

Few times of year feel as promising as the Wild Corn harvest. With stalks densely packed and twice head-height, you can get lost in a maze of abundance. The deeper you wander into the fields, the more colors you encounter: a glorious display of the well-fed winter to come. Because the availability of fresh corn is scarce when compared to the more traditional cornmeal we all use, I've included a recipe to maximize this seasonal treasure.

Grilled Corn, Pepper, and Onion Salsa
Serves four

- 2 Sweet Green or Red Peppers
- 2 ears fresh Wild Corn, any color
- 1 Yellow Onion, cubed
- 1 clove Garlic, minced
- ½ teaspoon Cumin
- 2 tablespoons Lime Juice
- 2 tablespoons Sunflower Seed Oil
- ¼ cup fresh Basil, chopped
- Salt to taste

1. Start your fire in the grill.
2. Rub oil on sweet peppers, husked corn, and skewered cubed onions. Cook all over direct high heat until soft, looking to lightly blacken the vegetable skins in places.
3. Peel, de-seed, and dice the roasted pepper. Cut corn from cob. Chop onion. Mince raw garlic.
4. Toss vegetables in bowl with remaining ingredients and mix thoroughly.
5. Serve over grilled fish, chicken, or pork; or with tortilla chips as a snack.

Golden Wheat

The grasslands east of the old Lantern Light Power Plant remain deeply hazardous, and even I won't spend much time there. A bit further down-valley, though, some remarkable things are happening. The alluvial plains have become a curious incubator, with Golden Wheat the primary beneficiary of circumstance. The modest glow it emits on the plate is both novel and strangely soothing. If you experience itchy eyes from eating Golden Wheat, take a couple days off before you try it again.

Golden Wheat Pasta Dough
Noodles are wonderful fresh and can be dried and served later
- 1½ cups Extra Fine Golden Wheat Flour*
- 1 cup Golden Wheat Flour
- 1 teaspoon Salt
- 4 large Egg Yolks
- 3 tablespoons Sunflower Seed Oil
- ½ cup Water

1. Combine flour and salt on a large cutting board and make into a volcano form. Add yolks and oil, working by hand into dough. If too dry, add one tablespoon of water at a time until desired consistency is achieved.
2. In batches, roll the dough into thin sheets on a lightly floured surface and cut into desired noodle shapes. Drape cut noodles around your workspace until the entire batch has been processed.
3. The pasta will be most tender if boiled and eaten the same day, though it saves well for future use once completely dry.

* Make your own Extra Fine Golden Wheat Flour by removing both the germ and the bran before grinding in your mortar and pestle.

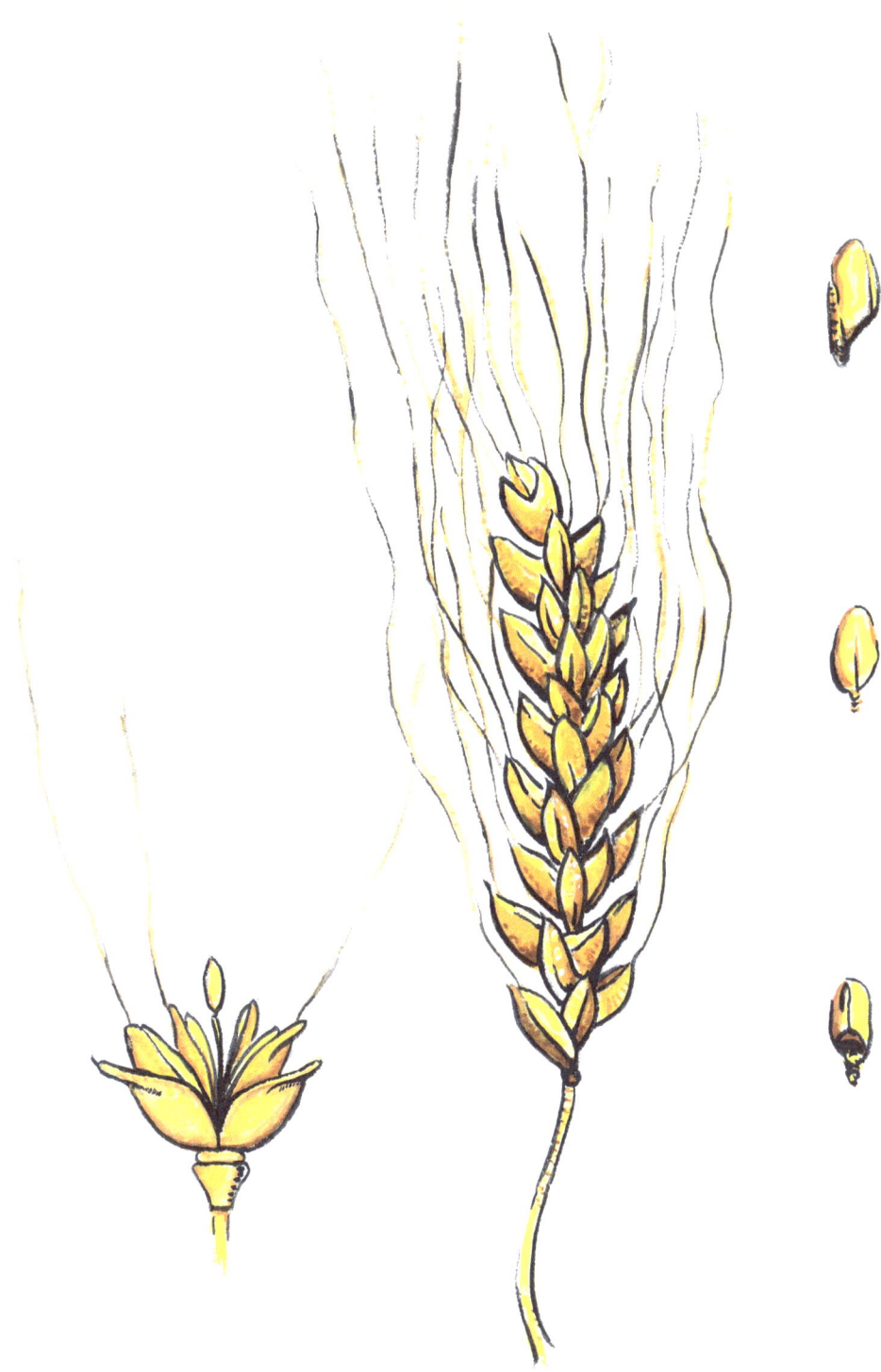

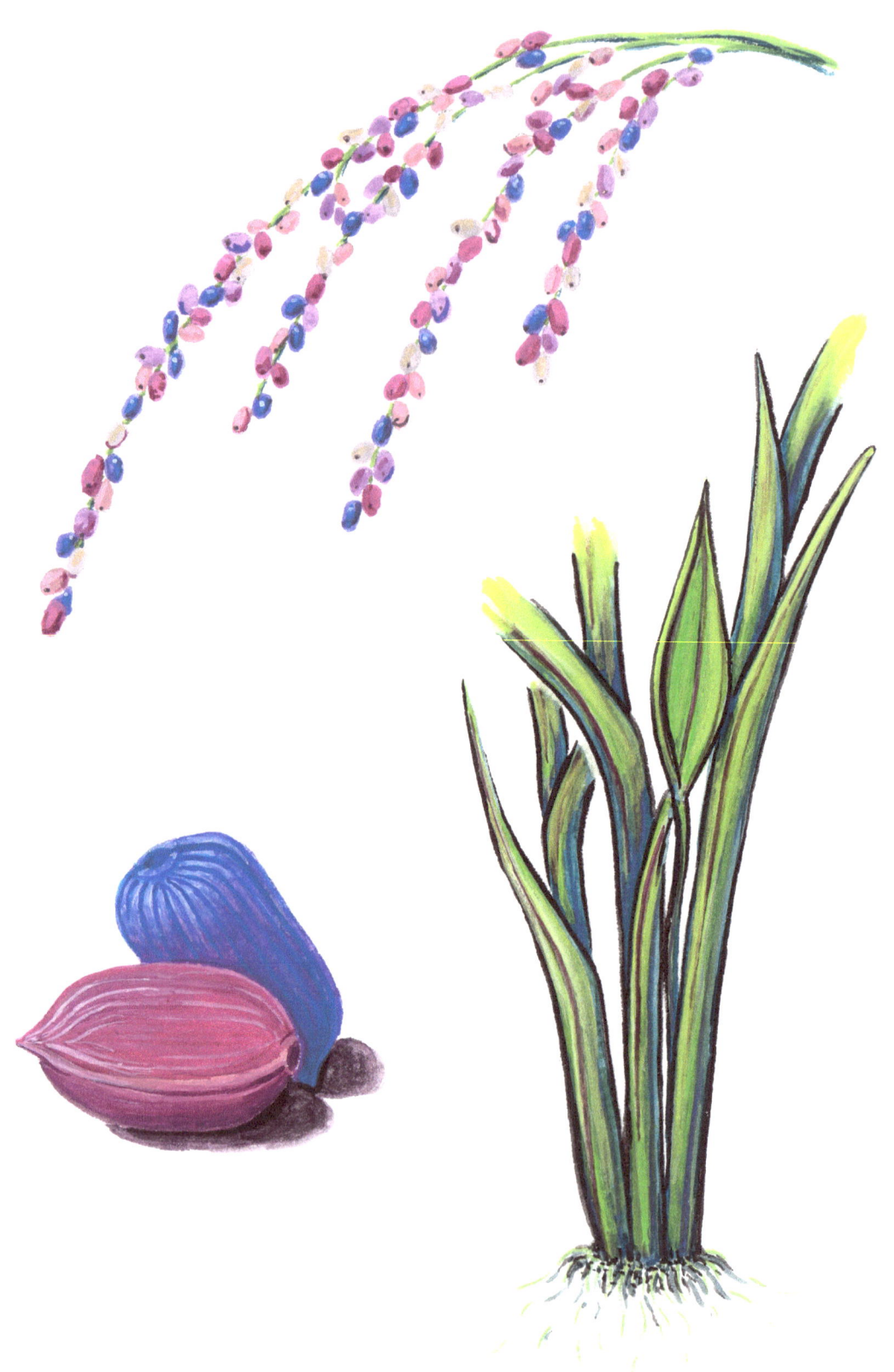

Wild Rice

This colorful grain adds a festive touch to any meal while also provid-
ing a great source of energy throughout the day. A centuries-old staple,
Wild Rice is a fitting side dish for breakfast, lunch, and dinner. Of course,
this means leftovers... Here's a simple and tasty dessert that utilizes the
cooked rice you already have on hand.

Rice Pudding
Serves four

- 4 cups Milk
- 2 Eggs
- 1 cup Brown Sugar
- 2 tablespoon Golden Wheat Flour
- ½ teaspoon Baking Powder
- ¼ teaspoon Salt
- ½ teaspoon Vanilla Extract
- 3 cups cooked Wild Rice
- ¼ cup dried Golden Weekenders
- 1 tablespoon Cinnamon and Sugar, mixed

1. Start a small fire in your grill.
2. Whisk together milk, eggs, brown sugar, flour, baking powder,
salt, and vanilla extract.
3. Bring to a boil in a medium pot, transfer to lower heat to simmer,
reducing liquid by half. Stir occasionally as mixture thickens, about
twenty minutes.
4. Add rice, weekenders, and the cinnamon and sugar blend. Cook
for another five minutes, allowing flavors to unite.
5. Can be served hot or cold.

Gemstone Potato

Sadly, many people still believe their wealth represents their value in this world. But what good is money when there's nothing worth buying? And how can a coin be more beautiful, or more useful, than a single Gemstone Potato? To think these tasty tubers are hidden beneath our feet—simple, wholesome, and available to all. Though digging them can be exhausting, the fatigue is forgotten as your basket fills. Store them cool, dark, and slightly dirty. You'll be saving the best for last: the magic moment when you wash them, revealing their mesmerizing, deep-purple skin and the promise of their buttery-flavored goodness.

Roasted Gemstones, Onions, and Ghostroot
Serves four
- 10 Gemstone Potatoes, quartered
- 1½ large Yellow Onions, cut into wedges
- 3 large Ghostroots, irregularly cut into 1-inch pieces
- 3 tablespoons Sunflower Seed Oil
- 1 sprig Rosemary
- Salt and Ground Picant to taste

1. Build substantial coals in the fire and move to one side for indirect heat.
2. Roll all the cut vegetables in oil, adding rosemary leaves, salt, and ground picant to taste.
3. Spread into single layer on a sheet pan. Place on covered grill and cook thirty minutes. Stir once and cook for another thirty minutes, or until golden brown and fork tender.

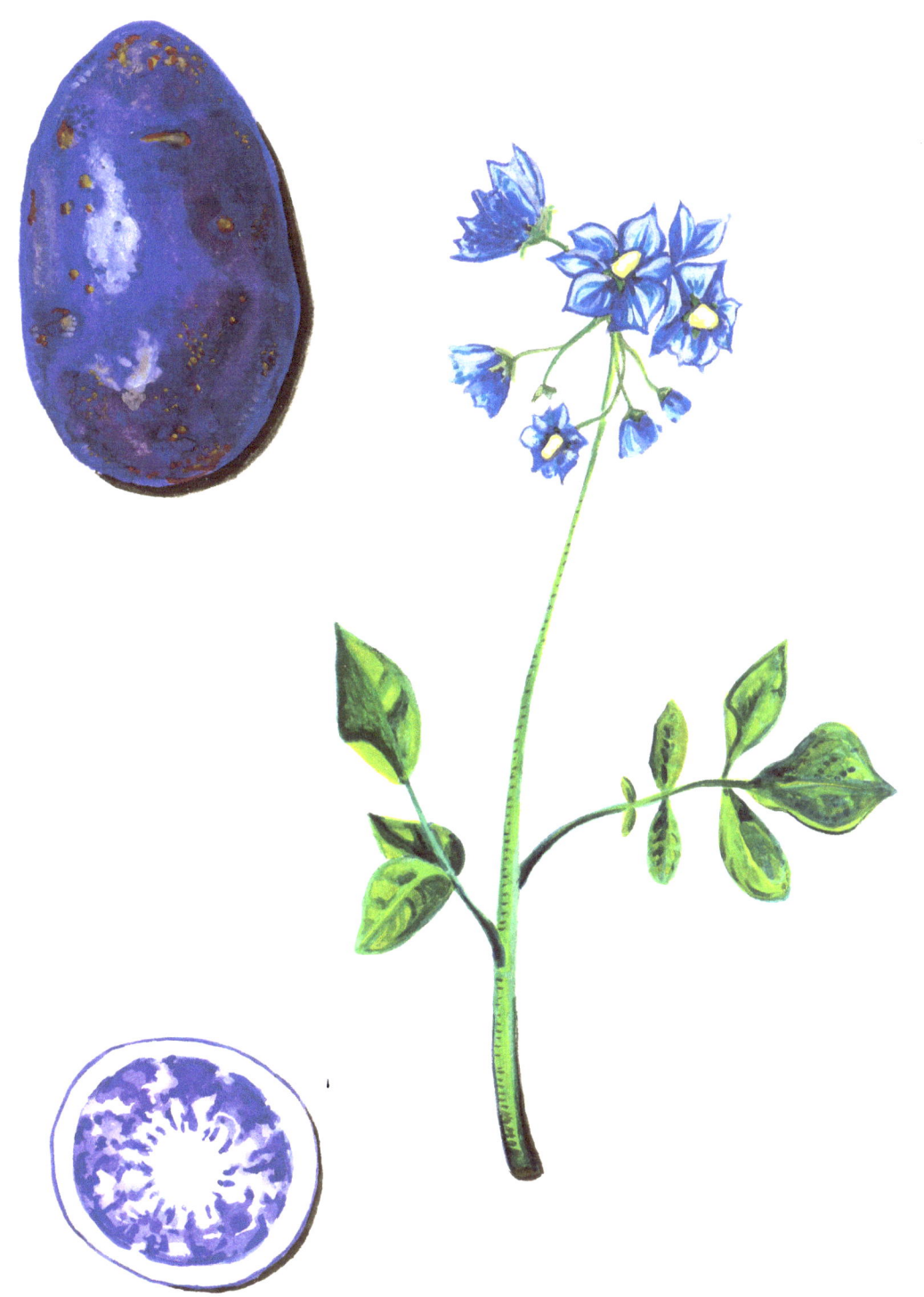

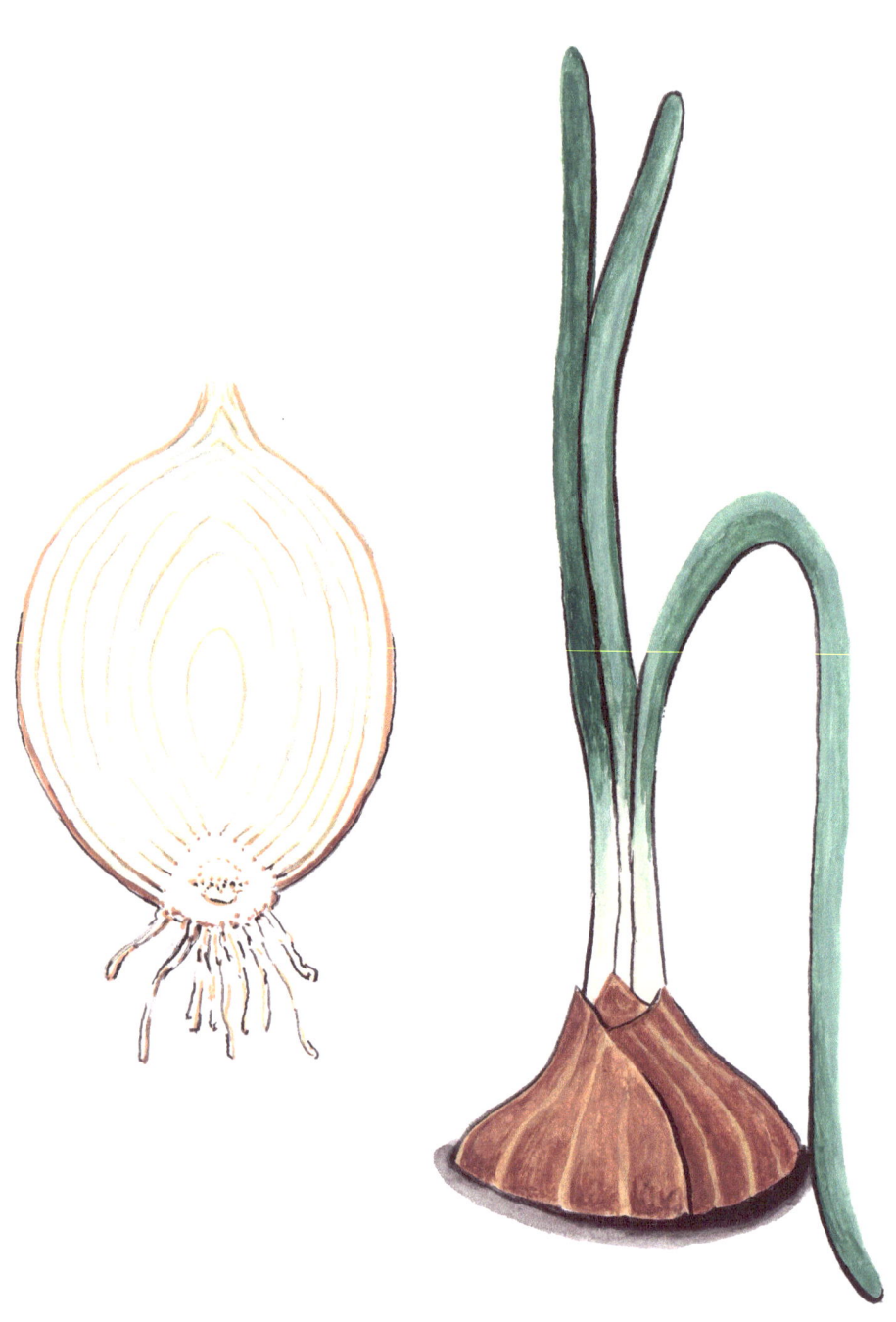

Yellow Onion

Sharp when raw yet sweet when cooked, Yellow Onions are a fitting symbol of our lives. Their versatility is astounding; their capacity to complement a variety of dishes makes them essential to your kitchen. Fortunately, they're hearty plants and can weather the early spring cold and the first fall frosts. They also keep well, so stock your pantry when you find them. The frittata recipe that follows is an equally flexible addition to your menu, a delight for breakfast, lunch, or dinner.

Yellow Onion Frittata
Serves four
- 1 large Yellow Onion, diced
- 3 tablespoons Butter
- ¾ pound Swiss Cheese, sliced
- 6 Eggs
- 1 cup Milk
- 1 tablespoon fresh Basil, minced
- 1 tablespoon fresh Lemoline, minced
- Salt and Ground Picant to taste

1. Start your fire and move coals to side of grill.
2. Caramelize onions in butter over low heat. The slower they cook, the softer and sweeter they become. Cook for thirty to forty-five minutes, if possible.
3. Line pie pan with Swiss cheese and set aside.
4. Whisk together eggs, milk, fresh herbs, salt and ground picant in a medium bowl and set aside.
5. Remove finished onions from heat and let cool.
6. Combine onions and egg mixture; pour into pie pan.
7. Grill covered over indirect heat until eggs have set. The middle will puff up. The frittata is ready when a fork lifts clean from the center.
8. Can be served hot or cold.

Ghostroot

The mythology surrounding this charismatic root vegetable is fantastic. Generations of children have been raised believing that Ghostroot only grows where gruesome battles have been fought. Their iron-rich color is an expression of blood spilt; their sweetness, proof of victory claimed. Though the story exists to keep children from wandering off unsupervised, sometimes I wonder if by glorifying our own capacity for violence, we aren't also guaranteeing theirs.

Mashed Roasted Ghostroot with Pesto-Greens
Serves four
- 2 pounds Ghostroot with tops
- 2 tablespoons Sunflower Seed Oil (for roasting)
- 2 tablespoons Butter
- ¼ cup Cream
- ½ teaspoon Ground Nutmeg
- Salt and Ground Picant to taste
- 1 clove Garlic
- 1½ tablespoons Walnuts
- ½ cup fresh Basil
- ¼ cup Parmesan Cheese, finely grated
- ½ cup Sunflower Seed Oil (for pesto)

1. Start a medium fire and prepare coals for roasting over indirect heat.
2. Separate ghostroots and tops. Select two cups of leafy green tops and set aside; coarse cut the ghostroot for easy handling when it's time to mash them.
3. Roll ghostroot in oil, spread on sheet pan, and add salt and ground picant to taste. Roast covered until golden brown and fork tender, about thirty minutes, turning them occasionally.
4. As ghostroot cooks, mash raw garlic and walnuts into a coarse paste with your mortar and pestle. Add basil, Parmesan, and reserved ghostroot tops; grind until an even texture is achieved. Add sunflower seed oil one tablespoon at a time as needed, whisking until combined. Add salt and ground picant to taste. Set aside.
5. In small batches, use the mortar and pestle to blend the roasted ghostroot until the desired texture is achieved. Work in butter, cream, and nutmeg.
6. Plate mashed ghostroot with a dollop of pesto-greens on top.

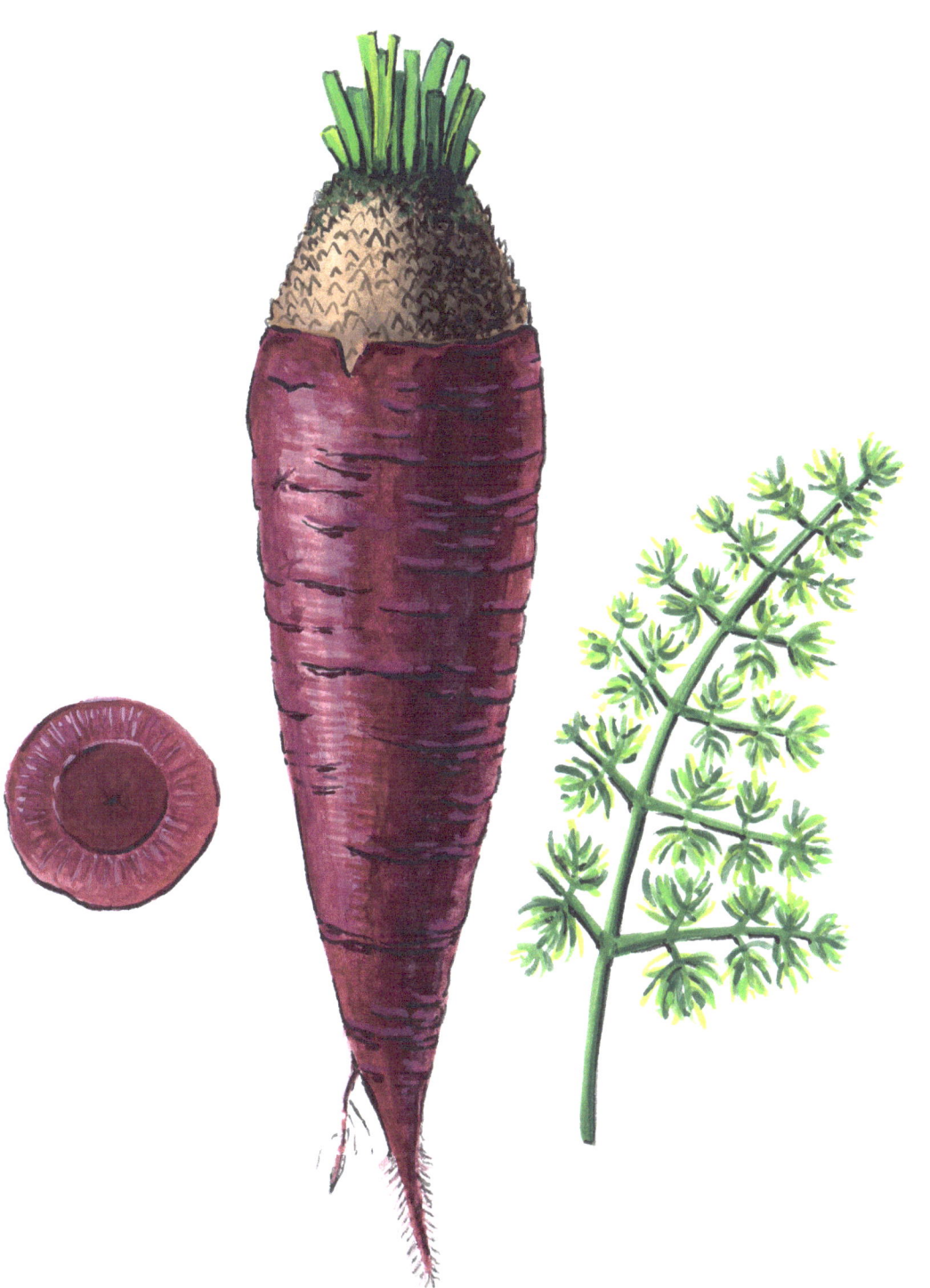

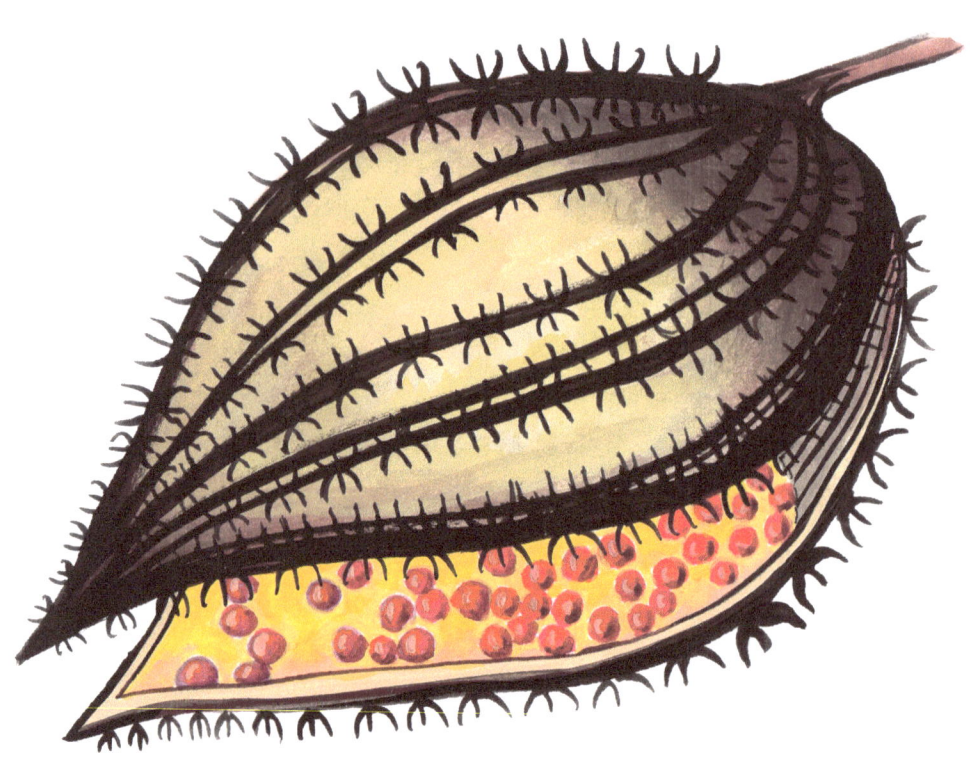

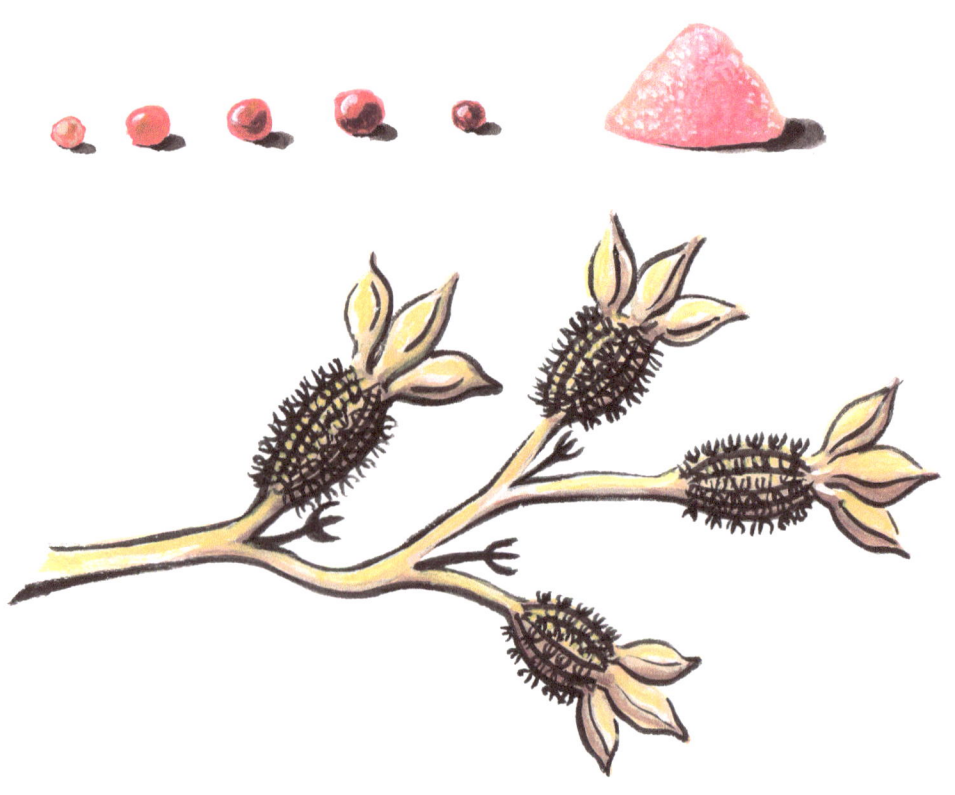

Ground Picant

This kitchen and field-satchel essential adds spice to any meal and luckily, there's no reason to ever run out. Ground Picant comes from a climbing vine that's perfectly suited to life on the chain-link fences surrounding abandoned commercial buildings and parking lots. Depending upon the season, try to select the most mature seeds to grind for use with your meals. Though still palatable if harvested while developing, the younger seeds are more bitter than bright in flavor.

Ground Picant Focaccia
Makes 1 large loaf
- 2 cups lukewarm Water
- 1 tablespoon Active Dry Yeast
- 4 tablespoons Sunflower Seed Oil
- 2 tablespoons Umbrella Mushroom-infused Sunflower Seed Oil
- 1 tablespoon Course Ground Picant
- 2½ teaspoons Salt
- 5 cups Fine Ground Golden Wheat Flour
- 2 teaspoons Rosemary

1. Activate yeast by mixing with lukewarm water in a large bowl.
2. Combine oils, reserving two tablespoons for later use. Pour the oil into the yeast with half of the salt and ground picant. Add the fine ground golden wheat flour in small batches, mixing by hand until a soft, sticky dough is formed.
3. Oil a second large bowl; transfer dough and cover with a wet rag. Allow dough to double in size, about an hour.
4. Prepare your fire, with intent to bake your focaccia at high heat.
5. Lightly oil a sheet pan and place dough on surface. Gently form the dough into a flattened, rectangular shape, matching the pan's dimensions. Texture the surface of the dough with your fingertips to create focaccia's characteristic shape, drizzle top with reserved mushroom-infused oil, and sprinkle the remaining salt, ground picant, and rosemary on top. Allow to rise for twenty minutes, or until coals are ready.
6. Bake covered until golden brown, about thirty minutes.

Sunflowers

I cannot highly enough recommend cultivating Sunflowers. They're beautiful. They grow vigorously, with little care required. The seeds are great for snacks, served on salads, and perhaps most important, their oil can be extracted and is an indispensable ingredient for a rewarding cooking experience. Anticipate that fabricating your press* will be a pain in the ass, but you only have to do it once, and your quality of life will be so greatly improved that it's time to quit complaining and just do it.

Cold-Pressed Sunflower Seed Oil

* Sunflower Seeds, in the quantity you have time to process

1. Start a small fire in the grill.
2. Collect, wash, and dry sunflower seeds. In small batches, mash with mortar and pestel until shells are broken open and meats are exposed.
3. Spread the mash on a sheet pan and roast over low heat, turning frequently. Remove from heat once shells begin to brown. Do not overcook.
4. Process the toasted mash with your cold press, collecting the oil for future use. The leftover husks and meats make wonderful birdfood, so cast it around your camp and enjoy the extra company.

* A cold press has three main parts: a perforated cylinder, a piston that moves within it, and a collection dish. Depending upon the materials you're able access, try to follow these tips when you make your own press. You'll want to have some way to anchor it, so look for a sturdy table-clamp or consider affixing it to a heavy base. If possible, the piston should descend from a lever arm, connected by a hinge to your perforated cylinder. If you site the hinge a few inches outside the cylinder's rim, you'll get a longer press arm, thereby increasing leverage and decreasing user fatigue. Also, consider making your collection dish removable so that transferring the oil you've produced into your storage containers is quick and easy.

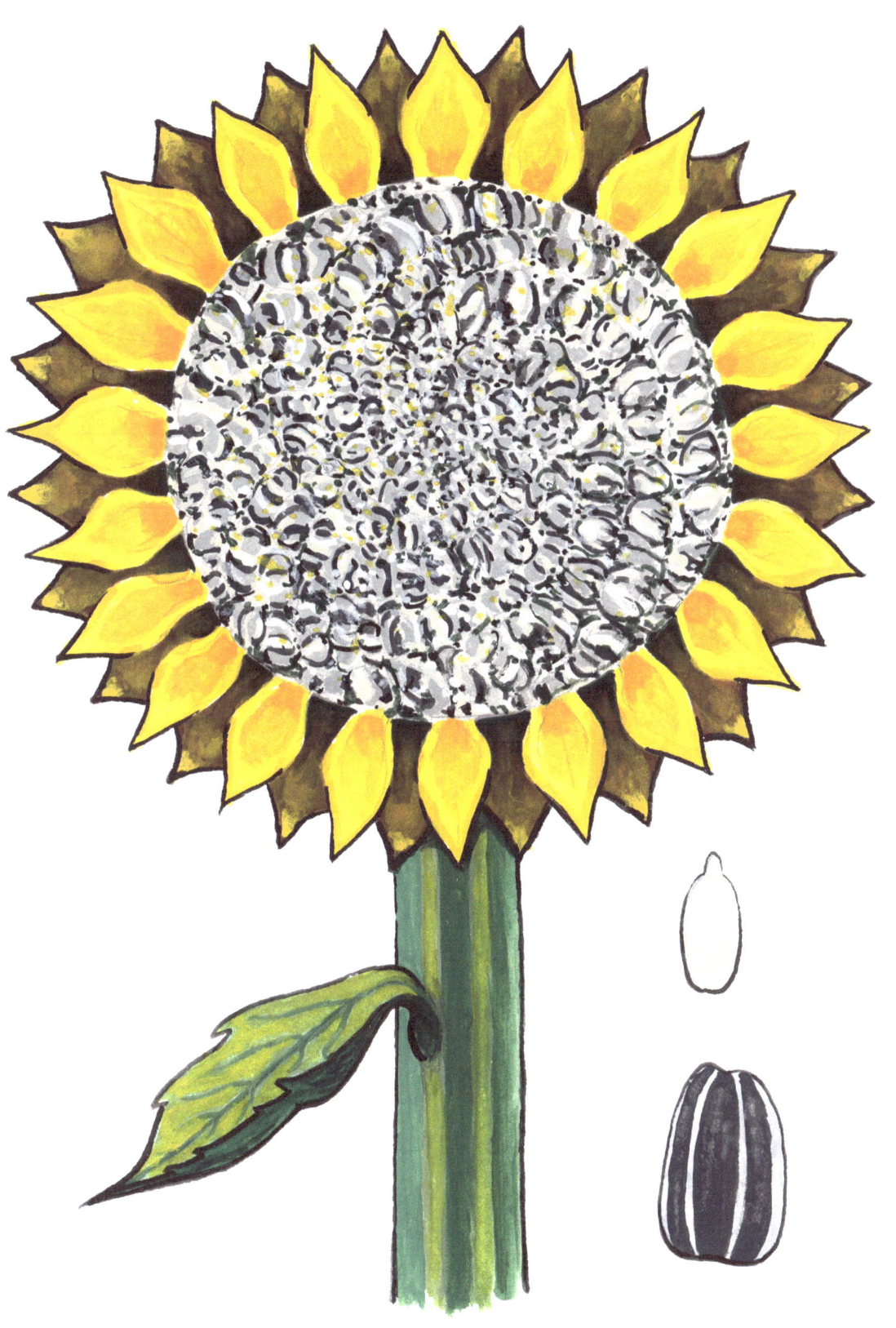

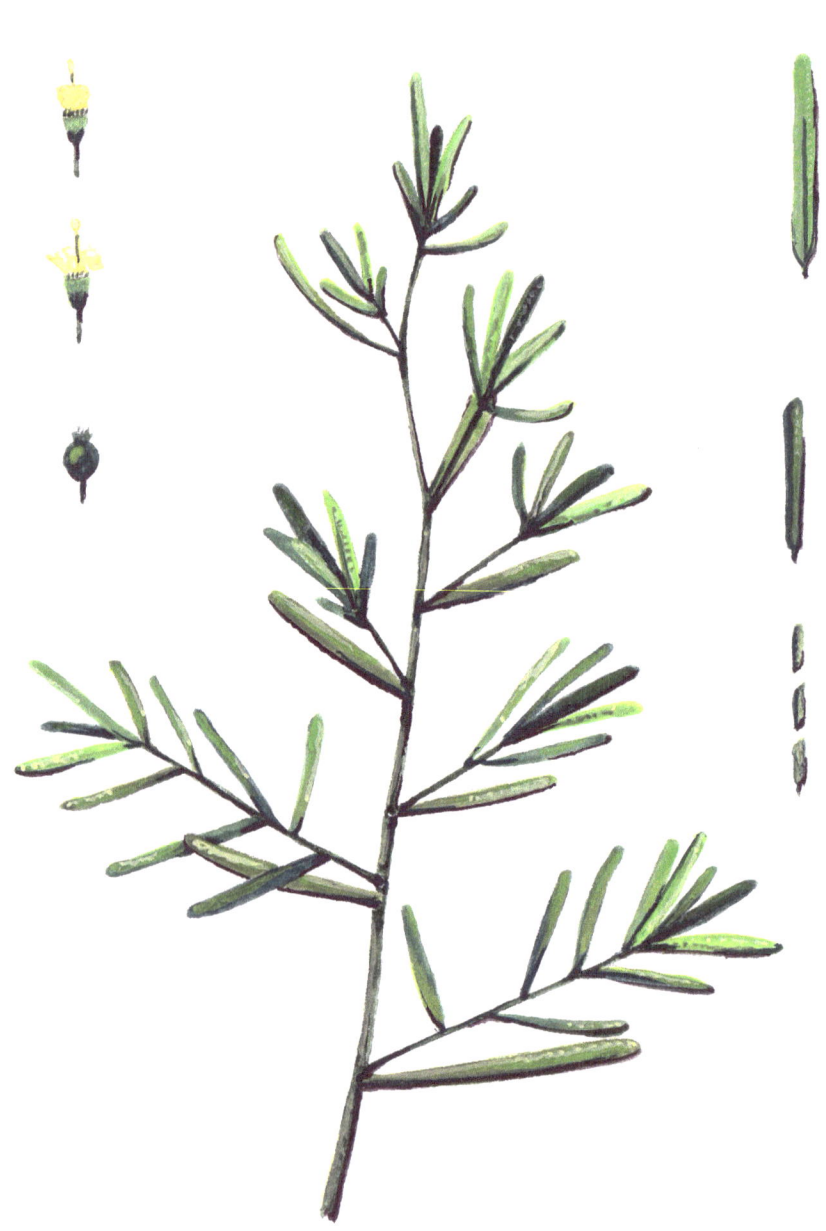

Lemoline

Lemoline's reputation as a central ingredient of Balthrovan cuisine precedes it, so don't be shocked if neighbors disparage it, and you, from a nationalist perspective. This sentiment is saddening and ridiculous, as Lemoline contributes a bright citrus flavor to any meal and its vivid-green color enlivens the plate. The plant's compact structure grows conveniently in window boxes, and its yellow flowers attract butterflies in late summer. What's not to like?

Baked Trout with Lemoline Butter
Serves four
- 4 tablespoons Butter
- 1 teaspoon fresh Lemoline, minced
- ½ teaspoon Lemon Zest
- ½ teaspoon fresh Parsley, minced
- ¼ teaspoon Sugar
- 4 Trout fillets, deboned
- Salt and Ground Picant to taste

1. The herb butter is best made ahead of time.
2. Allow butter to soften. Once workable, whip the combined herbs, zest, and sugar into the butter until thoroughly blended. Scoop into balls and place the individual servings on a tray. Once portioned, return the butter to your ice chest so it can set up once again.
3. Start low temperature fire on the grill.
4. Place trout fillets onto lightly buttered sheet pan and spice with salt and ground picant to taste. Cook covered on the grill until flesh is opaque and flakes begin to separate, about eight minutes.
5. After the fish has been plated, garnish with a small scoop of herb-butter. Lean a single sprig of lemonine on top of the butter for an additional flourish.

Red-Stemmed Spinach

The iron-rich leaves and stems of this annual are best when eaten young and tender. As they mature, they're equally good but benefit from being cooked. Red-Stemmed Spinach can be planted from April to September, yielding crops from May through October. The family recipe I'm sharing below was one of my grandmother's favorite sides. I remember gathering Red-Stemmed Spinach with her when I was a child, singing together at dusk, moving slowly through the cooling air before retreating to the warmth of the kitchen. Gone too soon, may she rest in peace.

Wilted Red-Stemmed Spinach
Serves four
- ¼ cup dried Weekenders
- 1 cup hot Water
- ¼ cup Sunflower Seed Oil
- ½ Yellow Onion, diced
- 2 cloves Garlic, minced
- 6 large bunches Red-Stemmed Spinach
- ½ cup Balsamic Vinegar
- ¼ cup Sunflower Seeds, toasted
- Salt and Ground Picant to taste

1. Reconstitute weekenders by immersing in a bowl of hot water for about twenty minutes. Remove when plump and set aside.
2. Over medium-high heat, sauté onions and garlic until dark brown and crispy. Pour in vinegar and reduce liquid by half. Add red-stemmed spinach leaves to pan and stir so they wilt evenly, quickly, and are coated in sauce, less than five minutes. Salt and ground picant to taste.
3. Transfer to serving bowl and top with toasted sunflower seeds and weekenders.

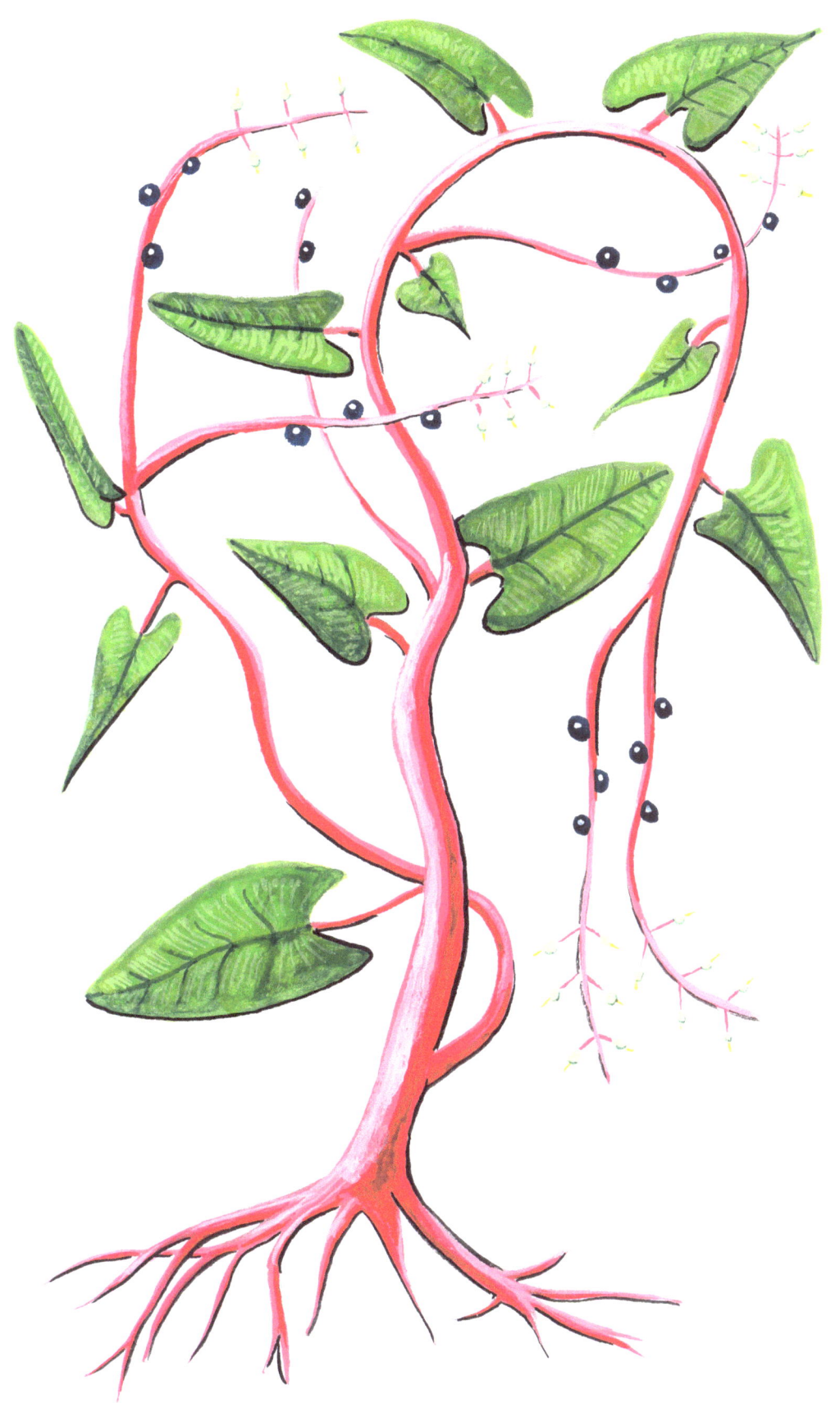

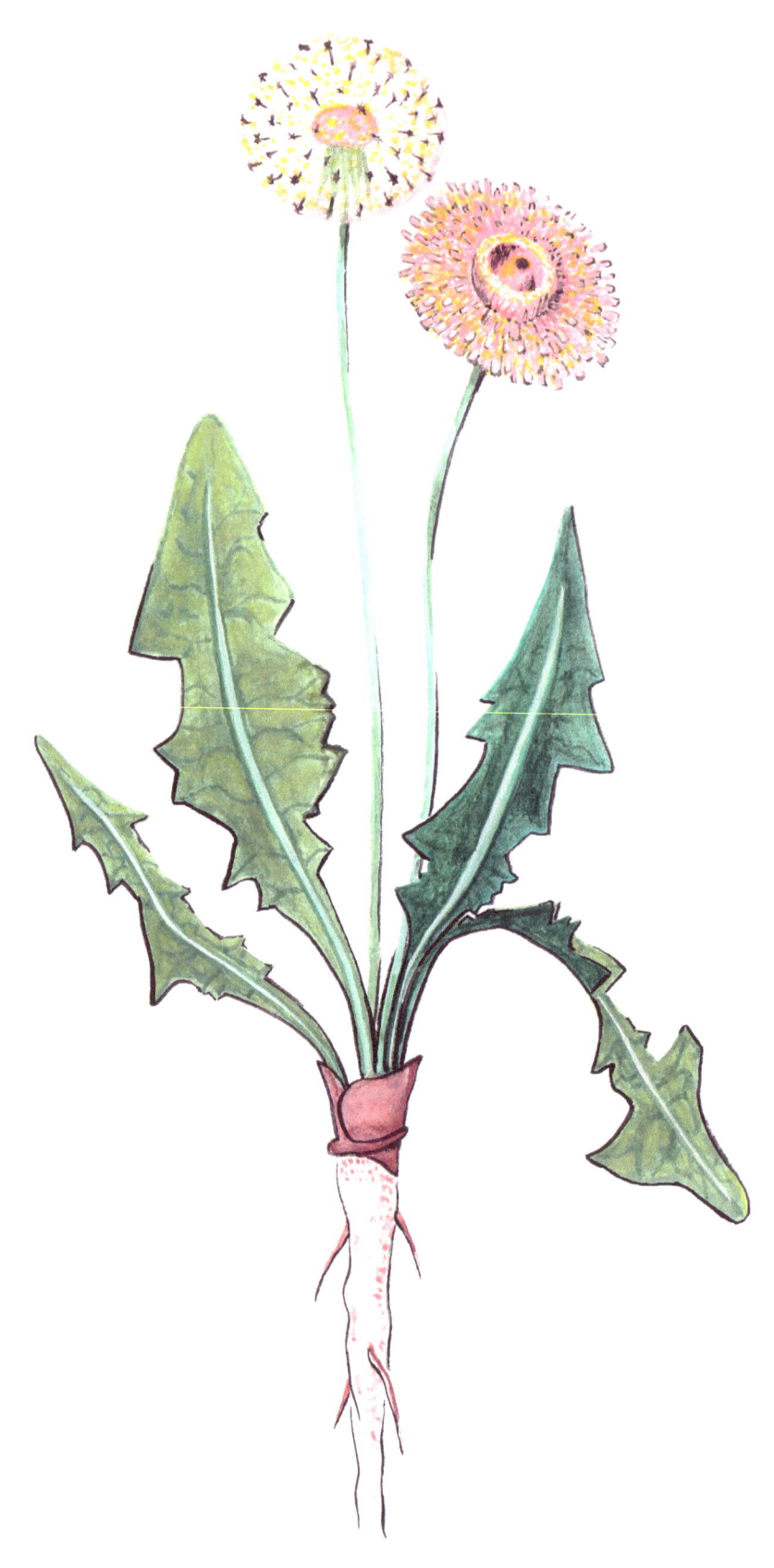

Dandelion

Loved by children and loathed by gardeners, one way or another Dandelions will always be in our lives. Primarily utilized as a medicinal plant, a tea can be made from the leaves and roots that stimulates digestion and detoxes the liver. The tacky, white sap is also a decent bug repellant, though few use it this way. Do remember that Dandelion pollen and nectar are essential, early-season components of bees' diets, so our future depends on them, too. Would you want to re-live the madness of the Hymenopteran Wars? Thank goodness the bees were able to drive-off their robotic replacements long before we were born.

Dandelion Dumpling Starters
Serves four

- 12 young Dandelion Flowers
- ½ cup Golden Wheat flour
- ¾ cup Wild Cornmeal
- ½ teaspoon Ground Traveler's Pepper
- Salt and Ground Picant to taste
- 2 Eggs
- 1 cup Sunflower Seed Oil

1. Heat oil in small pot over a medium-high fire.
2. Scramble eggs in a shallow bowl. Combine dry ingredients in a second bowl and mix thoroughly.
3. One at a time, dip dandelion flower in egg and then roll in the wild cornmeal mixture.
4. Once battered, fry the flowers in oil until golden brown. Remove from pot and let drain before plating.
5. Consider serving with Grilled Corn, Pepper, and Onion Salsa as dip.

Northern Squash

Northern Squash is the final harvest of the year, which means you're probably ready for a break from splitting and stacking wood when they're ready. But don't put away your tools—you'll need your hatchet to free them from their vine, and a wheelbarrow to get them home. Their wart-covered skin is alligator tough, so don't bother dulling your knife on one: besides, when else do you get to use a saw in the kitchen? Once cooked, the Northern Squash's dusty blue flesh reveals its relationship to the sweet summer melons, and it does look beautiful on the plate.

Stuffed Northern Squash
Serves four

- 1 Northern Squash
- 2 tablespoons Butter
- 2 tablespoons Yellow Onion, chopped
- ½ cup Goat Cheese, crumbled
- 3 cups leftover Meat and leftover Rice, chopped and mixed
- ½ cup Ground Picant Focaccia Crumbs
- Salt, Ground Picant, Thyme, Mustard Seed to taste

1. Start a medium-sized fire in your grill. This recipe does have a long cook time, so be sure to check and replenish the coals as you go.
2. Using a saw, cut a vent in the squash for steam to escape while baking. Cook covered over indirect medium-low heat for ninety minutes.
3. Meanwhile, combine onions and butter in a medium pot and sauté until the onions are translucent. Add leftover meat, rice, cheese, breadcrumbs, salt, grount picant, and spices. Roll together until ingredients are well mixed. Set aside and let cool while squash cooks.
4. Remove squash from heat when it is soft enough to quarter with a knife. Discard stem, seeds, and strings. Using a fork, further tenderize the light-blue flesh. Be careful not to break the outer skin, which doubles as a bowl to retain this meal's flavors.
5. Shape meat and rice stuffing into individual servings and position on top of the northern squash moons. Bake covered for another fifteen minutes, allowing flavors to unite.

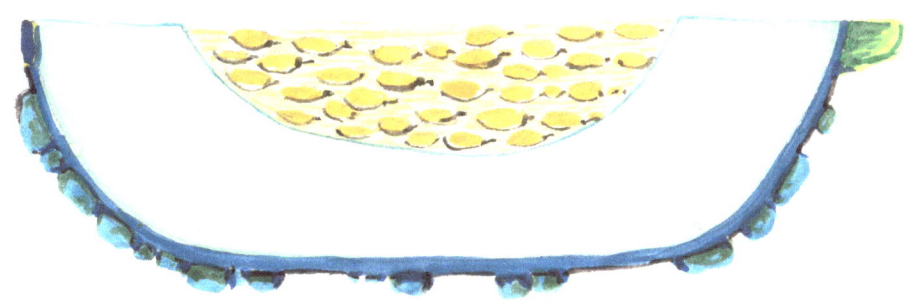

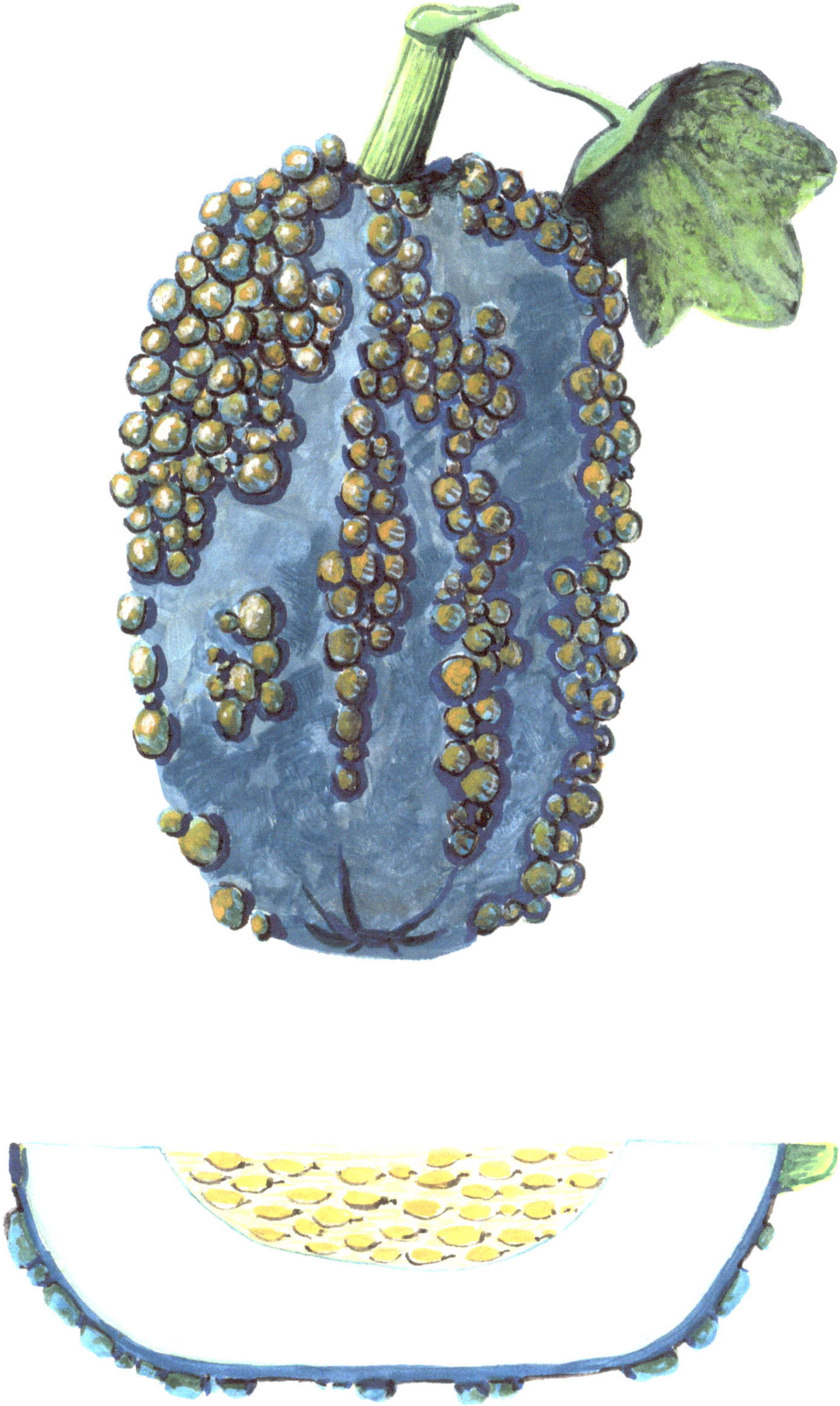

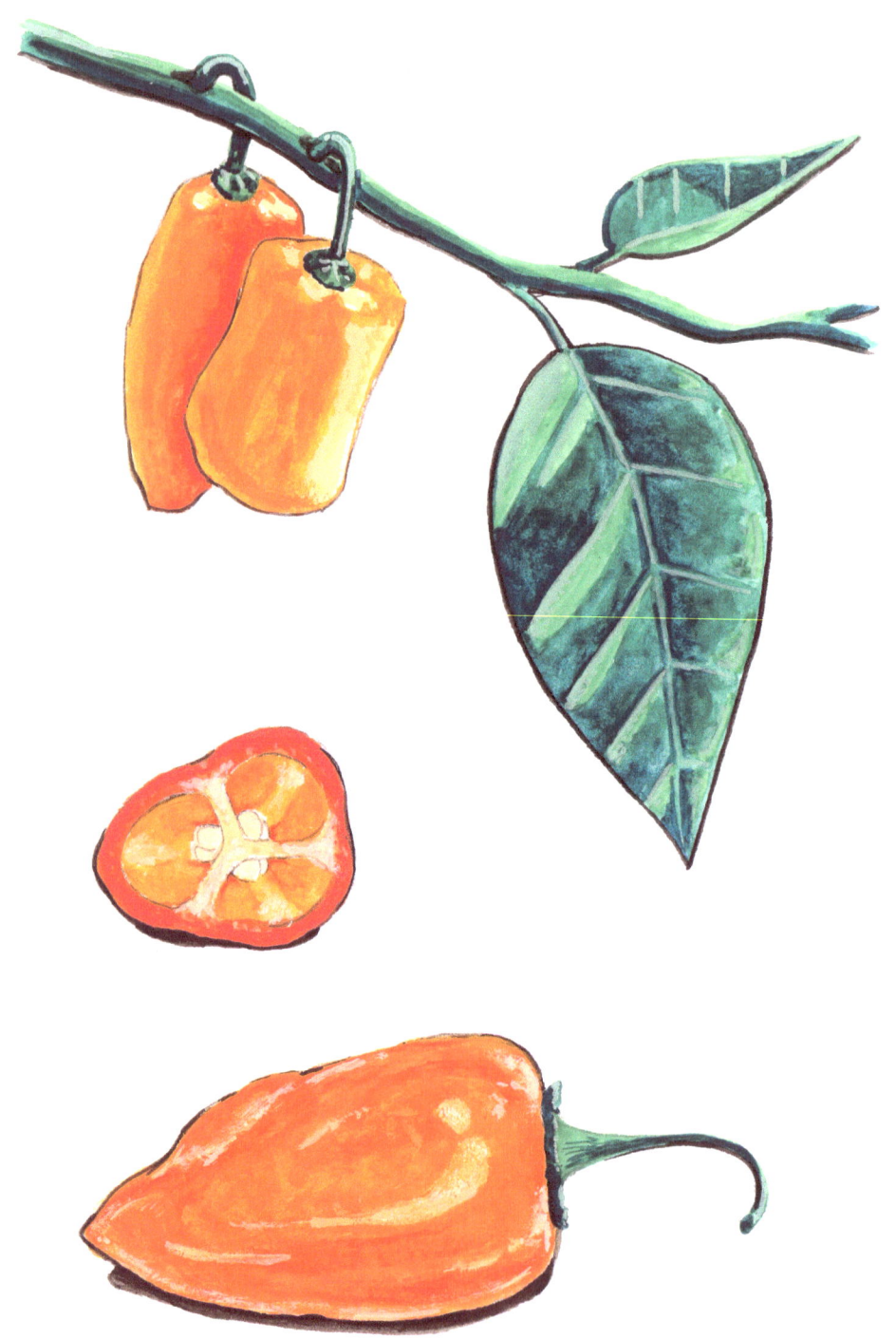

Traveler's Pepper

Few foods warm you up faster than the near-perfect spice of a Traveler's Pepper. You can feel it in your blood, a certain vitality circulating through your body, awakening and invigorating your entire system. The peppers transition from green to orange to red as they mature. Picking the peppers small and green yields the mildest flavor. They're hottest when the orange is waxy bright. And they attain a smoky flavor as the flesh softens, turning red. Remember to wash your hands after working with Traveler's Peppers and before going to the bathroom. Forgetting to can be really funny, when it happens to somebody else.

Traveler's Pepper Jelly

Makes four jars

- 1½ cups Water
- 3½ cups Sugar
- ¾ cup Apple Cider Vinegar
- 2 Limes, Zest and Juice
- 3 Traveler's Peppers, finely chopped
- 1 cup Winterfruit Pectin*

1. Making jelly requires a big fire and multiple large pots.
2. Combine water, sugar, vinegar, lime juice, lime zest, and traveler's peppers in a large pot. Set over high heat, stirring constantly. Allow to boil for three minutes before removing from heat. Add pectin. Return to low heat, stirring constantly for two more minutes.
3. Quickly transfer jelly into sterile jars and seal containers by boiling in an immersive water bath for another twelve minutes.
4. Consider serving traveler's pepper jelly on crackers with goat cheese for a starter or on grilled meats as a main dish.

* Wintefruit Pectin can be made by boiling down unripe winterfruit and should be done ahead of time. You'll need a large pot, eight cups of water, and sixteen winterfruit, quartered with stems, seeds, peels. Bring everything to a boil and cook uncovered until winterfruit have fallen apart and water has reduced by half. Strain all solids from the stock, return to heat, and further reduce down to two cups. Seal in jars for future use.

Sugarsweets

Sugarsweets are better prepared than raw, making them more of a year-round treat than a seasonal delicacy. Though poaching them in a sugar-water bath and drying them in the sun feels anti-climactic after an exhausting day climbing trees to pick them, it's essential to follow through with this extra step. With the additional processing, the flesh becomes sticky, tender, and sweet, and the skin achieves a crunchy, candied texture. Sugarsweets are fantastic when cubed and mixed with nuts for a mid-day snack, or more ritually, served on a platter with tea in the afternoon.

Sugarsweet Fritters
Serves four

- 2 cups Sunflower Seed Oil
- 1 cup Golden Wheat Flour
- ¼ teaspoon Baking Powder
- Salt to taste
- ¼ cup Pineapple Juice
- 15-20 Candied Sugarsweets, chopped into one-inch strips
- ¼ cup Coconut, grated
- ¼ cup Pistachio Nuts, chopped

1. Heat the sunflower seed oil in a deep pan over a medium-high fire.
2. Whisk together golden wheat flour, baking powder, salt, and pineapple juice to make the batter.
3. In a second bowl, combine coconut and pistachio.
4. One at a time, dip sugarsweets in batter, roll in nuts, and immediately drop into hot oil. Fry until golden brown.
5. Let rest to drain excess oil before serving.

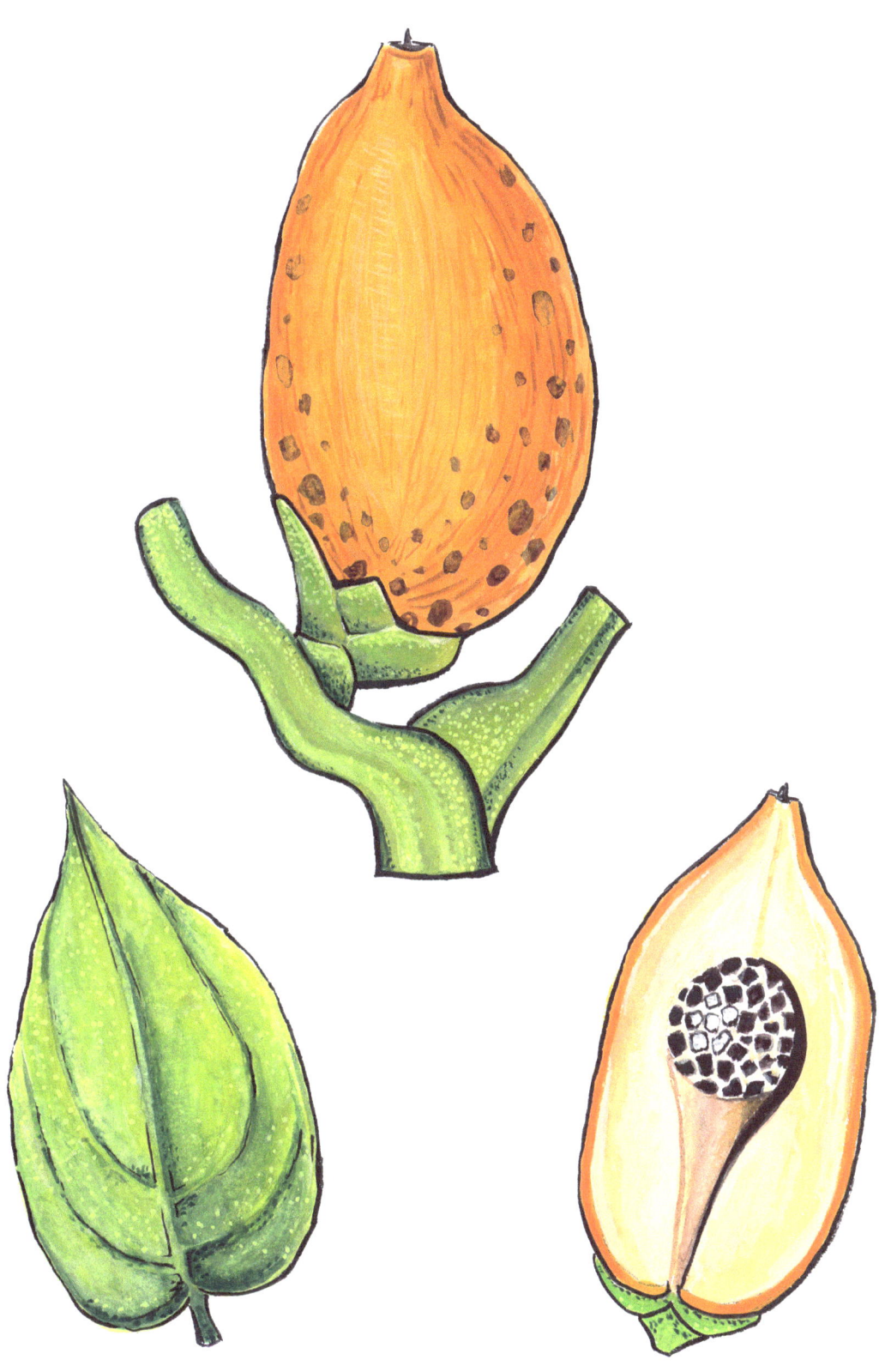

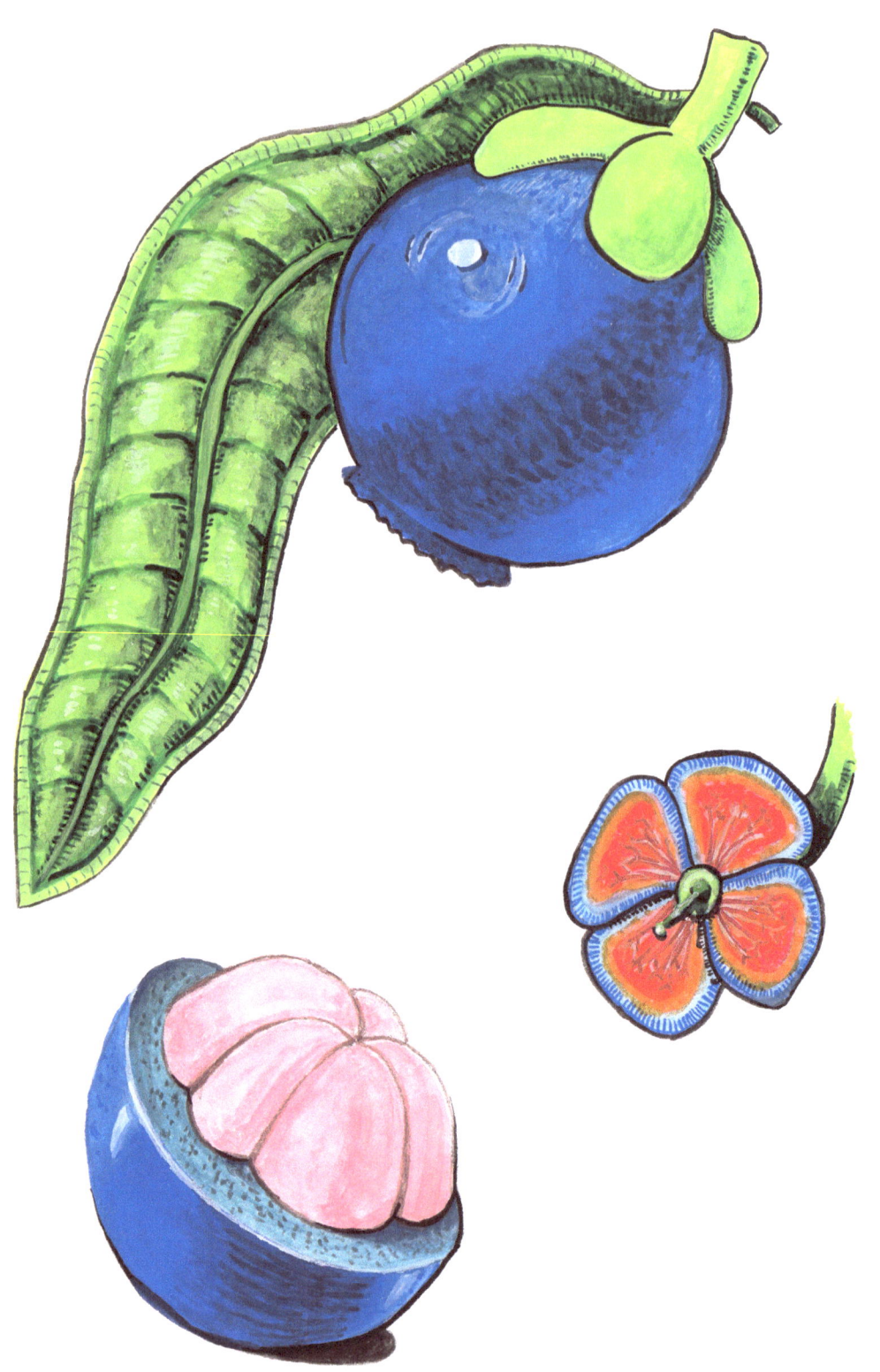

Bluetooth Berries

The Bluetooth Berry is a simple summer pleasure. If you find a patch, eat and eat and eat until your teeth turn blue, just like you did when you were young. Because the truth is, your mouth will be blue if you eat one or if you eat twenty—so you might as well stop everything, indulge with child-like glee, and then return to the task at hand. There will be no hiding that you were slacking off, as it can take two days for the blue stain to fade from your fingers and your teeth. In a pinch, Bluetooth juice can be used as ink for signing documents, drawing, or dyeing clothes, though it seems a shame to use them in these ways when the season is so short and they're such a special treat.

Bluetooth Sauce
Serves four
- 2 cups Bluetooth Berries
- 1 tablespoon Sugar
- ¼ cup Water
- 1 teaspoon Lemon Juice

1. Combine all ingredients except lemon juice in a small saucepan and set over a medium-low fire.
2. Stir gently. Allow berries to break at their own pace, releasing their juices into the pan. Thicken until all berries have burst and sauce coats the spoon. Add lemon juice and remove from heat.
3. Pour on pancakes in the morning, mix into your sundowners, or serve over cake and ice cream for dessert.

Winterfruit

Though Winterfruit are the kissing cousins of apples and pears, they cook and eat like tree-grown potatoes. Do try one raw just for the experience, for no matter when you pick them, they taste under-ripe and are slightly astringent. Their tart flavor and crisp body are especially popular in baked goods, where they make beautiful pies and tarts when sliced thinly and displayed in a layered pattern. If you don't live near an orchard and plan to start one for your camp, you'll want to grow a minimum of six Winterfruit trees. It will be a couple weeks of hard work, but your family will have them for generations.

Winterfruit Stew
Serves four

- ½ Yellow Onion, chopped
- 2 tablespoons Sunflower Seed Oil
- 1 pound Beef, cubed
- ¼ cup Golden Wheat Flour
- 2 Tomatoes, diced
- 2 cups Vegetable Stock
- 2 Gemstone Potatoes, cubed
- 3 Winterfruit, remove seeds and cube
- 1 tablespoon Lime Juice
- ½ cup Candied Sugarsweets
- Salt and Ground Picant to taste

1. In a large pot, sauté the onion in sunflower seed oil over medium heat until translucent.
2. Season cubed beef with salt and ground picant and roll in flour. Add prepped meat and tomatoes to the pot. Stir occasionally for about ten minutes, or until all sides of the meat have browned and the interior is still red.
3. Pour in vegetable stock and bring to a boil. Add winterfruit and potatoes, return to a boil and then simmer uncovered for about forty-five minutes.
4. Once stew has thickened and the meat, potatoes, and winterfruit are cooked, remove from heat and finish with lime juice and sugarsweets. Adjust salt and ground picant to taste.

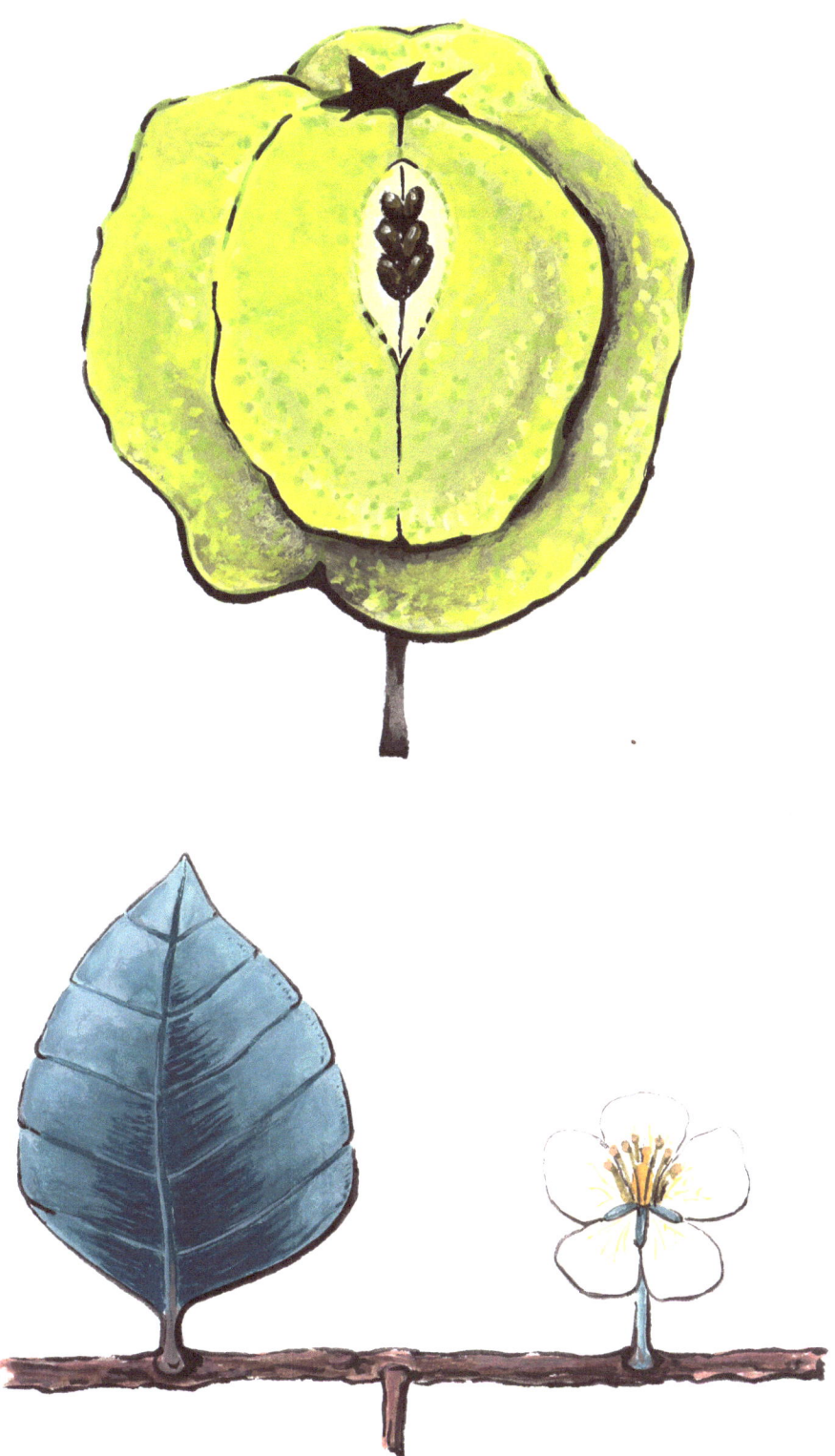

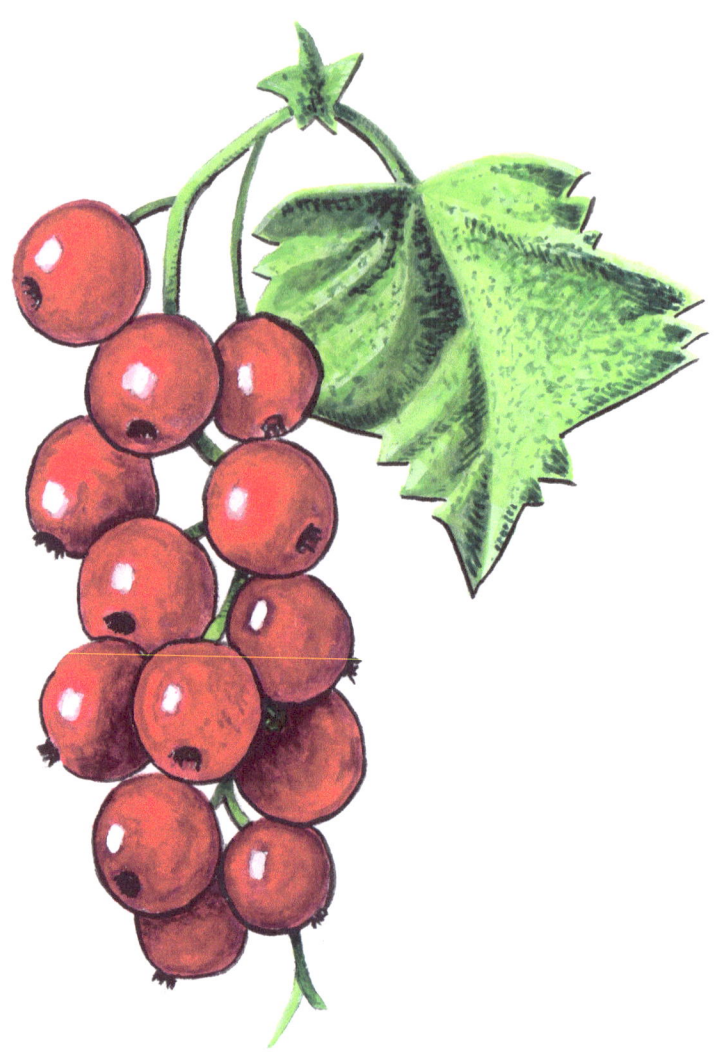

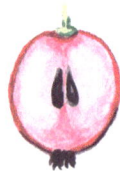 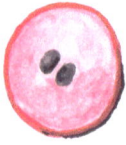 

Weekenders

Renowned for the wines they make, Weekenders will always be popular. Wherever they grow, people will thrive there, too—regardless of the difficulty. Weekender vines prefer mild winters, and though they only migrate two hundred yards a day, it can be a serious problem for the families that haul their belongings to stay close. Beyond victuals, the Weekender's delicate fruit is delicious straight from the vine, and kids love their juice on a hot day or dried as a snack between meals.

Roasted Gambler's Quail with Weekenders and Potatoes
Serves two

- 1 pound Weekenders, cut into small clusters and left on the stem
- 4 Leeks, cut into thin wheels
- 6 Gemstone Potatoes, cubed
- 1 tablespoon Lemoline, chopped
- 2 tablespoons Sunflower Seed Oil
- 2 Gambler's Quail, halved
- Salt and Ground Picant to taste

1. Build a medium-hot fire and shift coals to the side for cooking with indirect heat.
2. In a large bowl, combine weekenders, leeks, lemoline, potatoes, salt and ground picant. Roll all in sunflower seed oil and distribute evenly across the bottom of a shallow roasting pan.
3. Prepare halved quail by rubbing interior and exterior with Salt and Ground Picant. Nest the quail in the roasting pan, surrounding them on all sides by your fruit and vegetable medley.
4. Cook covered on grill for approximately forty-five minutes, or until quail juices run clear, skin is golden brown, and meat is white and firm to the touch.
5. Plate quail and serve fruit and vegetable medley as your side dish. Enjoy!

www.ingramcontent.com/pod-product-compliance
Lightning Source LLC
Chambersburg PA
CBHW050901180526
45159CB00007B/2747